Lucy Kemp-Welch
1869-1958
The Spirit of the Horse

Frontispiece: ***The Haywain.*** *Oil on board, 24in x 18in, c.1933. As a successful young artist, Lucy could not have foreseen the speed with which technology would undermine the horse-dependent world in which she had grown up.*

Lucy Kemp-Welch
1869-1958
The Spirit of the Horse

LAURA WORTLEY

ANTIQUE COLLECTORS' CLUB

ISBN 1 85149 252 6

British Library Cataloguing-in-Publication Data
A catalogue record for this book is available from the British Library

Printed in England by the Antique Collectors' Club Ltd. 5 Church Street,
Woodbridge, Suffolk on Consort Royal Matt paper
supplied by the Donside Paper Company, Aberdeen, Scotland

CONTENTS

Something in the Wind. *Watercolour, 21in x 27in. During the thirties Lucy focused increasingly on imagery which extolled the naturally free spirit of even working horses.*

ACKNOWLEDGEMENTS

I am most grateful for the encouragement I have received from John Kemp-Welch and members of the Kemp-Welch family, without whose continuous support this book would not have been written. Particular thanks for their help and enthusiasm are also due to Sally and Michael Carr, Sir Malcolm Field, Grant Longman, David Messum, Diana Steel and Diana McMillan of the Antique Collectors' Club, and Bing Taylor. Among the many other people and institutions who have also contributed information I would like to thank Ann Bressley, Nick Browne, The Hon Mrs Betty Clay, The Bushey Museum Trust, Tim Jeal, Paul Moyniham and the Boy Scouts Association, The National Army Museum, Lyn Roberts of the RNLI, Neil Roberts of Christchurch Art Gallery, New Zealand, The Royal Academy of Arts, London, and Bryen Wood.

PHOTOGRAPHIC ACKNOWLEDGEMENTS

The publisher would like to thank David Messum, of David Messum Fine Art Limited, 8 Cork Street, London for generously providing black and white photographs and colour transparencies of the works of Lucy Kemp-Welch that are illustrated in this book.

Thanks are also due to the following: J.M. Dent's 1915 edition of *Black Beauty*; The

Timber Run in the Welsh Hills. *Oil on canvas, 44in x 62in. Exhibited at the RA, 1932. Lucy had painted another Welsh timber hauling picture at Crickhowell near Lord Treown's home in Llanarth in 1928 and it is possible that this was set there too.*

Royal Collection © Her Majesty the Queen for 'The Clearing in the Forest', page 148; Imperial War Museum, London for 'Forward to Victory – Enlist Now', page 125, 'The Straw Ride: Russley Park Remount Depot', page 14-15 and 'Exercise', page 129; Phillips, London for: 'A Bad Place to Leap', page 35, 'The Brick Cart', page 61, 'If Only I Could Get Him Off', page 101, 'They Both Flew to her Head', 'Down!', page 188, 'It Was A Nasty Thing', page 184, 'It Was An Anxious Time', page 181, 'Wild Horses', page 206, 'Companions', page 91, 'My Early Home', page 178 and 'Now Auster Do Your Best', page 93; National Gallery of Victoria, Melbourne, Australia for 'Horses Bathing in the Sea', page 53; Bristol Museums and Art Gallery for 'Timber Hauling in the New Forest', page 25; 'The Waterway', page 76, courtesy of The Grundy Art Gallery, Blackpool; 'The Joy of Life', page 100, 'Barnet Fair', page 155 and 'Elephant Queen', page 158, courtesy of Bushey Museum and Art Gallery; Tatham Art Gallery, Pietermaritzburg, South Africa for 'The Village Street', page 69; Southampton City Art Gallery for 'Timber Run in the Welsh Hills', page 7; 'Women's Work in the Great War 1914-18', page 121, by courtesy of the Joint Grand Gresham Committee; Russell-Cotes Art Gallery and Museum, Bournemouth for 'Gypsy Horse Drovers', page 39 and 'Foam Horses', page 42; 'Sunlight Through Leaves', page 85, courtesy of Robert McDougall Art Gallery, Christchurch, New Zealand, presented by the Canterbury Society of Arts, 1932. 'Colt Hunting in the New Forest', page 43 and 'Forward the Guns', page 120 are housed at the Tate Gallery, London.

FOREWORD

The first time I became aware of my cousin Lucy Kemp-Welch and her painting was when, as children, my sister and I were both given a copy of *Black Beauty* which we loved and came to know well.

As our parents were friendly with Lucy, we did meet her occasionally. I remember her as a kind person, rather shy and deeply absorbed in her passion for painting and for horses. She was also modest and unassuming about her work, as is clear from correspondence with my father over a portrait of his two much-loved labradors in 1943. Due to the deterioration of her eyesight and the difficulties caused by petrol rationing, Lucy could only undertake to paint the picture from photographs and she was both apprehensive and diffident as to the final result. She need not have been troubled because her finished painting bore an outstanding and sensitive likeness to those two dogs that she never saw.

Rarely does a week pass without someone asking what relation I am to Lucy Kemp-Welch. As this is perhaps an indication of the continuing interest in and admiration of her work, I am therefore delighted to see a new book about her, containing so many illustrations of previously unpublished paintings.

The author describes how, at an early age, Lucy's picture "Colt Hunting in the New Forest" was a sensation, how it took the art world by storm, was bought for the nation and now belongs to the Tate Gallery. Her reputation as a painter went from strength to strength in the early years of this century, her illustrations for *Black Beauty* helping to make it one of the most popular children's books of all time. Possibly she became a victim of her own success, because having been lionised by the press and public alike in the earlier part of the century, she then declined into relative obscurity by the end of her life.

Whatever the reasons for this decline, I believe the text and the illustrations in this book demonstrate that Lucy's work can stand comparison with that of her peers, Munnings, Laura Knight, Cecil Aldin and Lionel Edwards – all currently better recognised than she. Thus I hope the book will not only help to add to the appreciation of those who already know her work but also introduce her paintings to a wider circle.

The book's publication has been a true team effort and if any member of the team had not made a full contribution, it would not have seen the light of day. Laura Wortley, who has built up an extensive knowledge of Lucy Kemp-Welch and her painting, has written an excellent text. David Messum, who, more than anybody else, has helped bring Lucy's work back into the public perception following the wilderness years after her death, has provided most of the illustrations. Diana Steel, of the Antique Collectors' Club, has produced and published a book of outstanding quality and it was Sally Slaney whose persistence got the project under way.

I am extremely grateful to them all, both individually and collectively, for their part in producing a book of which we can all be proud and which I believe is a fitting tribute to one of the outstanding painters of her generation.

John Kemp-Welch
October 1996

Young April. *Oil on canvas, 72in x 48in. Exhibited at the Royal Academy, 1910. This painting dealt with the complex relationship between young girls and their horses which Lucy had experienced herself. The insecurity of adolescence was mirrored in the horse's jittery fear of the imminent storm. Lucy worked on the idea for several years and the scale of the finished canvas allowed the figures to be almost life-size, increasing their impact substantially.*

CHAPTER ONE

"A Fair Start"

She Chose Me For Her Horse *(Black Beauty 1915)*

'Horses as Subjects'

If people remember Lucy Kemp-Welch today, it is invariably as 'the lady who painted Black Beauty'. She didn't make her mark on the world of art as an aesthetic innovator like Gwen John or Winifred Nicholson, or cast herself as an extrovert communicator like Laura Knight, or defy convention like Dora Carrington. She simply painted horses, but what horses and what feeling!

No one recollects the hullabaloo which greeted her painting 'Colt Hunting in the New Forest' when it was purchased for the nation in 1897, or the popular expectation in succeeding years that she must surely be the first woman Royal Academician for over a century. Few people recall her school, her vitality, her emancipation ahead of the suffragettes. How could they? She said so little about them herself. However, they know and love *Black Beauty – The Autobiography of a Horse* and when they visualise its dramas, more often than not the pictures which spring to their mind's eye are Lucy's.

To this day, her illustrations for J.M. Dent's 1915 edition remain the undisputed favourites out of the many alternative interpretations, including those by her colleagues Cecil Aldin (1912), Edmund Blampied (1922) and Lionel Edwards (1946).[1] In fact, her *Black Beauty* is more than just a favourite

1. *Anna Sewell: The Annotated Black Beauty*, edited by Ellen B. Wells and Anne Grimshaw (1989), p.xxxiv.

The frontispiece from *Black Beauty* illustrated by Lucy for J.M. Dent. Dent's daughter, Muriel modelled for the girl; Baden-Powell's horse, Black Prince, played the part of Black Beauty.

version; it was the best selling illustrated children's book ever and ran to innumerable subsequent editions, the most recent in 1986. In 1989, the authors of *The Annotated Black Beauty* selected Lucy's illustrations to accompany their text, favouring them above all other versions, both English and American. Yet incredibly, when Lucy undertook the project she had done hardly any illustrative work for fifteen years and would do even less afterwards. She was chosen for the commission purely on the virtue of her paintings, and it was as a *painter*, not an *illustrator*, that she tackled the project.

Painting, far more than illustration, involves active commitment to the subject. That Lucy always put painting and horses first, however, proved to be both her greatest strength and her greatest weakness, the reason for *Black Beauty*'s success and for her own obscurity. You would not think a horse painter could be forgotten in England of all places, where animals are so cherished and artists like Sir Alfred Munnings and George Stubbs so fêted.

This photograph, taken as she approached womanhood, emphasises Lucy's social timidity.

Yet Lucy was an intensely private and modest person. Even to the diaries which she kept for years, she confided few secrets. They record work, animals, domestic trivia and occasionally national events, but almost never personal feelings. When she set out rather haphazardly after the Second World War to tell her life story, she began not with her childhood, nor in the New Forest, but with her arrival as an art student in Bushey. And what she left out of that short text was revealing. It was not simply that as an artist she had acquired an unerring focus and Bushey set the action off at a cracking pace; it was that she considered her childhood would be out of place in a biography whose chief interest to others she presumed could be only the paintings and the horses. It never crossed her mind that she might be the heroine of her own story.

For Lucy, the heroes had always been horses. She was born in Victorian England, a society which was literally dependent upon horse power, not just for public and private transport but for the army, commerce, industry, agriculture, mining and forestry too. It would have been impossible then to imagine the world without horses and certainly there had never been a time at which they had not featured in Lucy's daily life, bringing the morning milk, delivering coal or pulling the governess' cart.

Her childhood too was almost totally circumscribed by her father's tuberculosis, and the animals which the children kept provided a welcome escape from the household's obsession with his health. Caring for horses, schooling and riding them, inculcates a sense of

The Straw Ride: Russley Park Remount Depot, Wiltshire. *Oil on canvas, 72in x 156in. Exhibited at the Royal Academy, 1920. For Lucy horses were always the heroes but* ***The Straw Ride****, painted at the end of the First World War, was also a celebration of women's intuitive handling of horses.*

responsibility while at the same time providing children with practical ways of expressing affection. A century ago horses also gave middle class girls a degree of independence, enabling them occasionally to explore their surroundings without a chaperone. There were many other excitements for boys, who cut the apron strings when they went away to school and thereafter could roam the neighbourhood freely. Even riding side-saddle, as was then customary, a woman felt uncharacteristically powerful. Although it is likely to be misconstrued

nowadays, this was an image beloved by Victorian novelists for feisty ladies, since riding apparently transforms a woman's relationship with her horse from being acceptably maternal into a partnership of masculine strength. In other words, for Lucy, at only five foot three, horse-riding represented strength and liberty.

The relationship she established with her ponies as a girl therefore was much more than a teenage passion; it was both intuitive bonding and release into a private world. It was an understanding so well-tuned that it would enable her

Sunset. *Pastel, 14¾in x 19in. Exhibited posthumously at the Pastel Society in 1959.*

to handle the fractious parade ground mount that even Baden-Powell rejected. Above all, it was fundamental to her later ability to paint horses with acute sensitivity yet without a trace of sentiment. Out of necessity, horses became a channel for her emotions and, though shy and modest in most things, where horses were concerned she was both articulate and bold.

It was this perhaps which first drew her to J.M. Dent's attention and the match he made between Lucy and *Black Beauty*'s author, Anna Sewell, was inspired. The two women shared an identity of interest and outlook which could never have been approached by a man. Just as Lucy was somewhat hampered by her invalid father, so Anna Sewell's activities were curtailed by her own chronic illness. To both of them, horses brought freedom and both enjoyed typically feminine and complicated relationships with their horses. In addition, there was a definite correlation in those days between the status of women and the status of horses in Britain, their roles so vital to the national infrastructure as to render them virtually invisible as individuals. *Black Beauty* had been intended primarily not as a children's story, but as a tract to promote reforms in horse management, and gender undoubtedly coloured, if it did not motivate, the perspective from which it was written.

A Clearing in the Forest. *Oil on canvas, 16in x 20in, 1924. Lucy's empathy for the plain-speaking shire distinguished her paintings from those of many, better known, male horse painters, such as Stubbs or Munnings.*

In the Dale Country, Bolton Castle. *Oil on canvas, 14in x 18in, 1910. Completed while Lucy was working on* ***The Riders*** *in Yorkshire, this is probably one of two oil paintings of the Dales included in Lucy's one man show at the Dudley Gallery in 1912.*

Significantly, although *Black Beauty* was told in the first person by a female author, for wider credibility at the time the horse had to be presented as male. He narrated a wide range of stories, his own and other horses', which corresponded uncannily to Lucy's experiences over the years when she painted horses variously as soldiers, labourers, mothers, performers and friends. In fact, she always went out of her way to court adventures which would bring other horses into her orbit and wherever possible she participated actively in her chosen scene so that she could paint how it felt to be involved, not just how it looked. It was this involvement which brought vigour and energy to her paintings and thus ultimately to *Black Beauty*. As she set about the task of illustration, memories constantly interposed themselves between her and the text, so that throughout the book visual allusions to her Royal Academy exhibits and other paintings abound.

Painting touches on feelings, illustration on fantasy and the distinction between them is what sets Lucy's *Black Beauty* apart from its rivals. Beyond the world of horses, many aspects of Lucy's private life, her spirit and independence, her vitality and sense of duty, her hopes and disappointments, had their parallels in Black Beauty's struggles. Yet unlike Laura Knight, with whom she has been compared, Lucy rarely wrote or spoke about her own feelings, although her paintings show her to have been extraordinarily perceptive about the feelings of her subjects. It is only when her paintings are read chronologically alongside her reticent diaries that patterns and emotions start to emerge almost

Lucy painting ***The Riders*** *on the Yorkshire Moors with Black Prince in 1910. The wooden case protecting the canvas in situ had to be anchored against the wall because of the prevailing winds.*

episodically. Lucy herself brought these together just once in her lifetime and then unwittingly, in her version of *Black Beauty*. With all its echoes and projections, the book is probably as close as she came to presenting a personal history and bound up within it tacitly, driving it forward, are the feelings which made her a remarkable painter of horses.

The Drinking Place in the Forest. *Oil on canvas, 16in x 25in. In Lucy's childhood some areas of the New Forest were still almost uncharted. As an adult she returned to explore them, hiding patiently with her sketch-books among the trees and bracken to catch glimpses of the secret Forest life. She began this picture there in August 1901.*

CHAPTER TWO

"My Early Home"

In Double Harness *(Black Beauty, 1915)*

'Horses as Family'

Lucy was eight years old when *Black Beauty* was published in 1877 and her father, Edwin Buckland Kemp-Welch, brought a copy of the first edition home. It would be graceful to say that the book made a lasting impact on her but truthfully the diagnosis of her father's pulmonary tuberculosis the same year had more far-reaching consequences for Lucy and her future. He had been a partner in the family firm of solicitors, Watt and Kemp-Welch, in Poole when Lucy was born on 20th June 1869 but he was always delicate and the tuberculosis led to his retirement when still in his forties.

Lucy's only sister, Edith, was born in 1870 and the young family lived in Bournemouth, first at Beaumont and then at Branksome Terrace. The girls were educated at home by a series of tutors. Their routine was quiet, structured, disciplined, and to Lucy in retrospect these days were happy and free. She must have been an unusual child, earnestly practising her music without prompting before breakfast and with a passion for gardening which never left her. Already venturesome and single-minded, as a little girl she would creep out of the sleeping house in the middle of the night to water her flowers.

There was church every Sunday and visits to their widowed grandfather,

Lucy's illustration for Chapter V, in which Black Beauty is given his name and first partners Ginger in pulling the carriage.

Bluebells in the New Forest. *Oil on canvas, 10½in x 15½in. Rambling with their father through the ancient Forest was a favourite pastime for Edith and Lucy as children.*

Martin Kemp-Welch, who lived at 'Woodlands' on the outskirts of town at Upper Parkstone. Their unmarried aunt, Janet, presided over the house with its distant views across wooded hills to the sea and the children often called in to show them their latest drawings. Even at six and seven, Lucy's notes to her father, who spent long periods in Scotland for his health, were filled with details of their various pets. With no other siblings and few playmates apart from second cousins whom they saw occasionally, the menagerie constituted their extended family.

In about 1879 they moved to 'Dinmore', a larger house in Branksome within walking distance of their grandfather's home. The girls were sent to a private school run by Mrs and Miss Slade at Faringdon House on the Poole Road. Both teachers and new friends were apparently impressed, the teachers by their lively intelligence, the friends by their originality. Tales were told of how they buried dead mice and birds in the garden and dug them up later to study the skeletons. Perhaps Lucy knew that the young George Stubbs had done this with horse carcasses and it was certainly more diverting than her father's botany and zoology textbooks, which she ploughed through on her own.

Their favourite pastime, however, was rambling in the New Forest with their father. At this period, before the advent of the Forestry Commission, there were still some areas of the Forest which were impenetrable and virtually unexplored. It was a haven for wildlife and Lucy's father, a keen amateur

Lucy painting ***The Forest Stream*** *for Canon Valpy in the New Forest with her dog Podger. The picture was begun in August 1899 and finished in 1901.*

naturalist and entomologist, encouraged the girls to hunt out and record its many plants and insects. It was apparently a place of superstition and smugglers too, but for Lucy the symbiosis between the ancient Forest and its ponies was the paramount attraction. An old wives' tale had it that New Forest ponies were descended from the horses which swam ashore in 1588 from the foundering ships of the Spanish Armada, but wild horses had roamed the Forest long before Canute or William the Conqueror. During Lucy's childhood 'Commoners' still actively exercised age-old rights to pasture ponies in the Forest and 'Agisters' and 'Verderers' oversaw the management of the herds and woodlands. In spite of having been run at various times with thoroughbreds and arabs to improve the stock, the New Forest pony with his short neck and sturdy shoulders is closely related to other indigenous, British, moorland breeds. Foraging year round on the scrubby heathland has made them tough, surefooted and resourceful. Lucy, who was similarly small and agile, found both the ponies and their home compelling:

> "The New Forest again supplies a type of little horse which has for me a fascination beyond words and the Forest itself feelings deeper than tears – great aisles of huge, grey trunks, dim transepts beyond in the twilight, with its pillars rising up into the still, green, darkness overhead, away from this green temple of silence, away into the laughing sunshine on the moorland beyond, with the stretches of bracken shimmering white in the

The Standing Beech. *Oil on canvas, 9½in x 16½in, dated 24 July 1893. Family ties brought Lucy back to the New Forest regularly for holidays while she was a student.*

summer sun with scattered herds of ponies feeding – a mile away another stretch of beech and shining white against the living green a forest monument to the centuries that are gone – a great dead beech tree standing as straight and as firm as when the Conqueror stood beneath it in its youth but crumbling slowly more like a stone. Listen, there is

Summer Drought in the New Forest. *Oil on canvas, 96in x 48in. Exhibited at the Royal Academy, 1896. An exercise in observation which Lucy undertook on Herkomer's advice in 1895 as preparation for painting* ***Colt Hunting in the New Forest*** *the following summer.* *(Present whereabouts unknown)*

Timber Hauling in the New Forest. *Oil on canvas, 118in x 58in. Exhibited at the Royal Academy, 1904. Painting at Foxhills during July and August 1903, Lucy turned her attention from New Forest ponies to heavy horses.*

> something moving. I sink into the bracken and wait. A little Forest family comes by along the track made by generations of unshod feet in single file. Now is the time to observe; the little grey patriarch (sic) in front with mane hanging to the knees and a spray of dead bracken entangled in it, that is the great-great-grandmother of the clan with her children and their children's children to the third and fourth generation. See they all partake of the same colour, the same strong family likeness and all confidently follow that little wise grey head. Ah how it strikes me, this Forest life."[2]

Although her father was proud of Lucy's talent, he was adamant that she should not pursue art, or anything else, as a career. In his view, painting was just a polite accomplishment for young ladies. Their mother, Elizabeth, however, was more encouraging. She had given them their first drawing lessons herself when they were tiny and continued to employ visiting art mistresses at home after they were sent to Faringdon House. Inevitably, horses were Lucy's favourite subject and what she had not seen for herself, horse races and hunting for instance, she was happy to imagine. She was an artist by instinct, taking her sketch book with her wherever she went in case something caught her eye and she said later that she couldn't remember a time when she had not felt the need to draw.

At fourteen she was showing work in local exhibitions and as a birthday present her mother sent her for a week to study animal physiology with a vet and family friend, Mr Goodall. A knowledgeable zoologist, whose natural

2. Lucy Kemp-Welch papers.

Sheep and Lambs Grazing. *Watercolour, 6in x 10in. Lucy's affinity with animals, acquired as a small child, dictated the course of her future career.*

history collection later found its way into the Museum at South Kensington, Goodall ran the Christchurch Hospital for Sick Horses where Lucy was already a regular visitor. He used his patients to explain anatomy to her but, rather than watch the sick animals, Lucy preferred to copy from Goodall's prints. These may well have included Stubbs' engravings for *The Anatomy of the Horse* (1766) over which he had laboured too, as a young man, making highly detailed drawings as he slowly dissected the decomposing bodies layer by layer.

Two years later Lucy received from a dealer in the town her first commission, a study of horses' heads in oil paint. By this time she had had a few lessons with Arthur Batt, a painter who lived in the Forest at Lyndhurst. She seems to have studied with Arthur H. Davies in Bournemouth for several months too, but as yet she had never had any structured art tuition. Meanwhile, her grandfather died just before Christmas 1884 and her father's health was steadily

Cattle by a Stream. *Chalk, 6in x 9in. A sketch for Raphael Tuck's* Farm Pictures, *1936.*

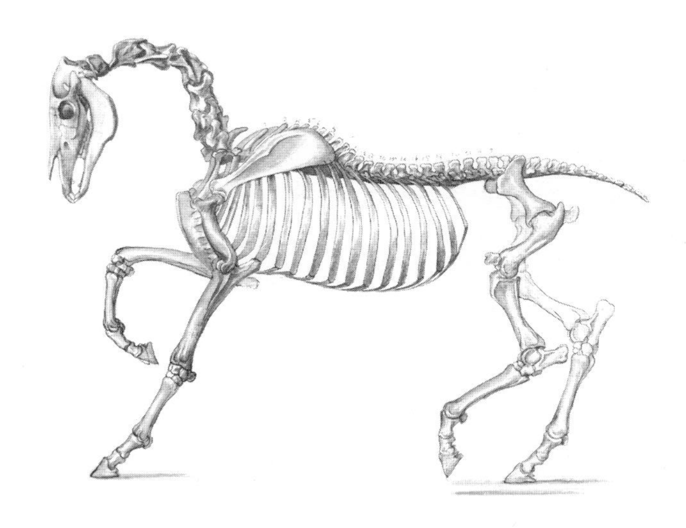

An early anatomical drawing.

deteriorating. 'Woodlands' was sold, Aunt Janet moved and it fell to Lucy and Edith to support their mother through the difficult period leading up to their father's death. Within months of his dying in 1888 their mother's health also broke down, and in 1890 they were forced to follow Aunt Janet to Weston Super Mare.

It was in the midst of this turmoil that Lucy's chimera of becoming an artist was suddenly transformed into reality. Her aunt heard that a distant cousin of about Lucy's age, Margaret Kemp-Welch, was studying art at Herkomer's school in Bushey, Hertfordshire, and she suggested that Lucy and Edith should try for places there too. Although only opened in 1883 with thirty-two pupils, the school had already gained a reputation for innovative teaching. Prospective students had to show "proficiency in drawing the head from life" before Herkomer would admit them, but with Aunt Janet's enthusiastic support the girls set rapidly about building up the necessary portfolios. They persuaded all and sundry, from the gardener to their tiny toddler cousin, to sit for them. The last of these paintings at least survives, now entitled by his descendants 'Grandfather When He Was A Little Girl'. Full of hope, the two girls eventually sent their applications off, only to be rejected. The piecemeal character of their previous art education had let them down.

Bird's Nest. *A juvenile watercolour showing the detail Lucy's father liked.*

Herkomer wrote, advising them to spend some time at a local art school to improve their drawing technique before re-applying. In spite of the disappointment, they took his advice to heart and, as they still had family affairs to settle in Bournemouth, returned to the School of Art there. Determined to succeed this time, Lucy began charging 5 guineas each for the portraits which would help improve her skills, striving to be as professional as possible. The fees at Bushey were 18 guineas a year and during the next couple of terms she earned over £60. When she and Edith re-applied in 1891, they were accepted at once.

Waiting to Pounce. *Paper on panel, 3¾in x 6in, 1887. This tiny study of a cat may be Lucy's earliest extant oil painting.*

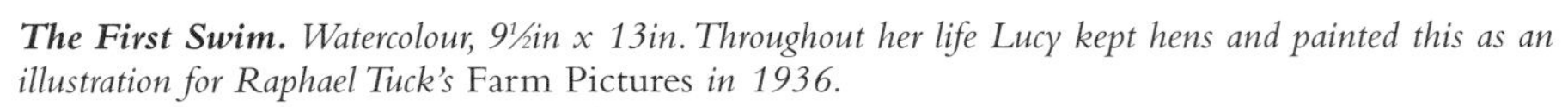

The First Swim. *Watercolour, 9½in x 13in. Throughout her life Lucy kept hens and painted this as an illustration for Raphael Tuck's* Farm Pictures *in 1936.*

***Bushey Church and Pond**. Watercolour, 6½in x 10½in, 1910. Lucy's arrival at Hubert Herkomer's school in Bushey in 1892 marked a complete change in her life and opened new horizons for her.*

Nevertheless, their struggles were by no means over. In the autumn of that year they set off for Bushey, possibly accompanied by their mother, a normal arrangement at the time for girls studying art away from home. Other sources maintain that their mother stayed in Weston Super Mare. Whichever it was, no sooner had the girls found comfortable lodgings a few minutes from the school, than their mother had a relapse and they had to pack up again. To add insult to injury as far as Lucy was concerned, during the week they had been in Bushey only Edith attended the school as Lucy had been in bed with a bad cold. Their mother died in February 1892 and it was not until April, six months after her first arrival, that Lucy finally set foot in Herkomer's school.

The bohemian atmosphere and high spirits of the students were the complete antithesis of the constraints the sisters had known before. The incessant family worries which had dogged their adolescence evaporated and they were caught up in a whirl of activity. The colony was dominated by the gargantuan personality of Hubert Herkomer, who was on one hand as generous and paternalistic as he was on the other autocratic and self-centred. By the mid-

Tired Out. *Oil on panel, 8in x 10in, 1891. As early as 1891, instinctively, Lucy was utilising the contrasted pairing of white and bay horses which would in due course become her hallmark.*

1890s nearly two hundred artists had made their homes around his school in Bushey which had until recently been a simple, rural community. Now the village and its inhabitants featured regularly on the walls of the Royal Academy as models for the social realist pictures made fashionable by Herkomer and Frederick Walker.

Herkomer's versatility and his expansive energy, so dynamically different from her father's personality, were a further revelation to Lucy, who fell quickly under his spell. His artistic talents encompassed not just portraiture and painting but wood-carving and silversmithing, as well as inventing new methods of printing and engraving. He did not hesitate to hold his own life up as an example to his pupils, extolling his rise from humble origins as the son of an impoverished German wood-carver to the ranks of the Royal Academicians by dint of hard work, and he swept the colony up in his infatuations with elaborate stage productions, music and even film-making.

Given the conventions of the time, there were probably few places in Britain

Lamplight. *Oil, 1890. Tired horses provided a theme to which Lucy would return many times.*

Foresters. *Watercolour, 9in x 13in, 1903. Lucy always wrote of New Forest Ponies with great affection: 'The New Forest again supplies a type of little horse which has for me a fascination beyond words and the Forest itself feelings deeper than tears...A little forest family comes by along the track made by a generation of unshod feet in single file. Now is the time to observe.'*

more promising than Bushey for two naïve young women to adjust to such new found independence. More particularly, under Herkomer's auspices there was no question of art not being a suitable occupation for a woman. From the school's inception he had tried to balance male and female students equally, although he refused entry to married women or women over twenty-eight, a standard condition at the time. His message, contradicting Edwin Kemp-Welch's, was that art should be regarded not as a frivolous pastime for women but as a serious commitment equal to a man's. To this end, two scholarships for men and two for women were offered annually at the school. Having suffered himself at the hands of repressive art teachers in both Germany and England, Herkomer rejected the "gigantic wholesale tuition" of the national art schools. He was determined that in his school pupils would achieve results through encouragement and he set himself to find and develop their talents individually, irrespective of gender.

Herkomer's theories about education might have seemed revolutionary, but his methods were rigorous and authoritarian. From his students he demanded dedication and an undertaking that they would study with him for at least a year. Though many students went in awe of him, and some girls evidently had crushes on him, others found his histrionics comic and articles on Bushey were

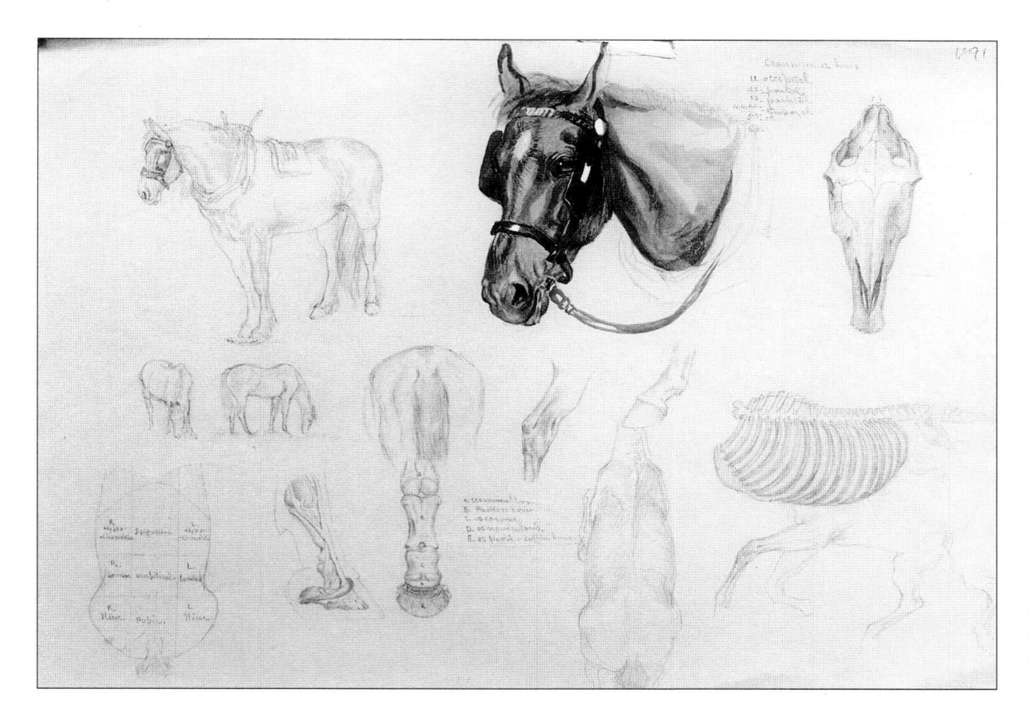

Lucy may have copied early studies like these from Mr Goodall's textbooks at the Hospital for Sick Horses.

as likely to be found in *Punch* as in *The Magazine of Art* or *The Studio*. Lucy, accustomed to self-discipline from childhood and bereft of a father, had no problems with either the hard work or the ego. She was at last being challenged to do what she had always wanted and she found Herkomer's enthusiasm infectious. For her, and for many of the girls at Bushey, he deserved their respect. He was the first man to take them seriously. She was twenty-two, financially independent and, unusually for a woman of her age and generation, her future would be of her own making.

The White Mare. *Oil on canvas, 7in x 5½in, inscribed Aug 26 '96. A preliminary study for* ***Colt Hunting.***

CHAPTER THREE

"The Hunt"

A Bad Place to Leap *(Black Beauty, 1915)*

'Horses as Youth'

Herkomer's school had a strange beginning. One day a Bushey neighbour, Mr Eccleston Gibb, asked him to give his niece 'a few lessons'. Nothing could have been further from Herkomer's idea of art education than a few lessons for a dilettante, so at first he excused himself pleading lack of time. Later on however, bizarrely, he suggested that if Gibb would build and fund a school for fifty pupils, men and women, he would give his services to all of them for nothing.[3]

There were only two classes at Bushey, the Preliminary supervised by Herkomer's assistant, Daniel Wehrschmidt, and the Life Class which Herkomer directed himself. Hours were long for all the students but differed between the two classes and according to summer and winter timetables. Few excuses for absence were accepted and students going AWOL could find themselves expelled. As in most art schools, tuition centred upon mastering the human figure. Preliminary students were put to painting and drawing the head from life, using casts for the complete figure, while the Life Class worked from live models all the time. When the model was nude, men and women worked in separate rooms to avoid embarrassment. The poor model, who was posed by the

3. For references to Bushey School, see Grant Longman, *The Herkomer School 1883-1900* and *The Herkomer Art School and Subsequent Developments, 1901-1918.*

Black Beauty's brother Rob Roy was killed after a fall during the hunt in Chapter II. Lucy made her name painting a colt hunt, unusually from the animals' perspective.

students, was given a ten minute rest every hour but the day was in all seven or eight hours long.

Lucy had been at Bushey two years before she came dramatically to Herkomer's attention. Her own memory was that she had not yet been promoted from the Preliminary Class although she had already ventured to submit a little picture done in the New Forest to the ROI. She had not had the chance to do any animal painting for months:

> "But on one memorable day...I saw from our front window a long procession of horses of all sorts and types going up the muddy road, no doubt to Barnet Fair a few miles off. They were shepherded and driven by wild-looking gypsy men on horseback, with frequent rushes to prevent the outliers from getting through the gates or turning up the side lanes. Never was there such an opportunity. I rushed from the house, gathering up my palette and a bit of something to paint a sketch on – this turned out to be part of the wooden slide out of my paint box – and ran after the procession which had now halted at a bit of green by a public house before going up the long, steep hill. There I made a lightning sketch of the scene – my long training of quick sketches in the street helping greatly."

Undaunted by her inexperience, Lucy envisaged her composition on a grand scale and had ordered a canvas 8ft x 4ft for it when she caught measles. She had planned to paint the picture in a large, rented studio but was now confined to her lodgings in Albert Cottages at the bottom of Clay Hill. When at last she embarked on the painting during her convalescence there was hardly room for the canvas, let alone herself or an easel, in the tiny sitting room. The picture had to be leant against the stacked up furniture and wedged through the open door into the passage.

Every week Herkomer held a 'Crit' session in which students could bring him work they had done in their own time for his advice and it was to one of these that Lucy brought the half-finished 'Gypsy Horse Drovers'. As she was short and the canvas large, some men friends had volunteered to carry it in for her and set it up in front of the Professor. Being in the Preliminary Class, Lucy had never come to Herkomer's personal attention before, and in the pause which followed, having no idea whether the painting was good or not, she became horribly embarrassed by its size. It grew bigger and more presumptuous with every passing second and she waited for the storm to break.

Herkomer's silence, however, betokened astonishment, not horror, and he finally asked who had painted it. His astonishment increased when the diminutive Lucy stepped forward, and on hearing she was in the Preliminary Class, he growled that she had better stay there for the present. But the next term she was promoted to his Life Class. Herkomer was so impressed by 'Gypsy Horse Drovers' that he advised Lucy to send the finished picture to the Royal

Heading off a Drive of Ponies. *Watercolour, 9¼in x 13¾in, 1896-97. Another by-product of* ***Colt Hunting,*** *this watercolour relates to an oil painting exhibited at the ROI in 1898.*

Academy. "I accordingly sent it," she recalled modestly. "It was well hung, but did not so far as I know attract any particular attention. That was in 1895." In fact it was sold before the exhibition even opened to Sir Frederick Harris for £60 and the copyright was bought by the Fine Art Society. To Lucy at that time it was success beyond her wildest dreams.

She was eager to continue with animal painting and her Hampshire cousins, the Mooring Aldridges, suggested the perfect subject for another large canvas, the autumn drift or round-up of the ponies in the New Forest for branding and sometimes selling. Herkomer tried to restrain her, feeling that she needed more experience before tackling such an ambitious project, but nonetheless she spent most of the long summer vacation of 1895 in the New Forest, scouting out the land and observing the ponies. At least one picture from this visit, 'In the Depths of the Forest', was a commission for which Lucy charged £5, while another, 'In the Marshes', was sold later that year at the ROI exhibition for 12 guineas. The most important product, however, was 'Summer Drought in the New Forest', which was shown at the Royal Academy the following year. Although it was another huge canvas, Lucy had acknowledged Herkomer's wisdom and did not attempt to depict the ponies in full flight. Instead she had caught a troop of mares and foals grazing unawares in a glade, conscientious groundwork for the more exacting subject she had in mind.

Study for ***Summer Drought.*** *Oil on canvas, 4¼in x 7in, 1896. Illustrated in the* Magazine of Art*, September 1899 where it was entitled* ***A New Forest Foal.***

In the summer of 1896 she returned to the Forest again, this time actively planning and preparing for the colt hunting picture. She made innumerable small oil sketches of foals, mares and stallions galloping from every angle and with different lighting effects. She never used a camera for any of her work and was convinced that her picture would only ring true if she took part in the drift herself. As an onlooker she had only been able to see excerpts of the action and the composition was throwing up questions which no-one else seemed able to answer.

She arranged to meet the colt hunters, all men, six miles into the Forest and rode on with them for several miles until, from a piece of rising ground, they caught a glimpse of a herd of shaggy ponies, tiny dots of colour on a heather covered plain. The men gave Lucy a long whip and suggested she start the chase so she trotted down gently towards the grazing animals. Then, breaking into a gallop, she circled round them, cracking the whip, and the little ponies took to their heels, fleeing for their lives.

Their speed over the rough and treacherous terrain was formidable but the pursuit was on and the hunters followed through ditches and hollows, across bogs and up hills, never slackening speed. For one brief second in the marshes Lucy could see no way through until the rider ahead of her made for a narrow plank and their horses dashed over it fearlessly, water and mud splashing up all around. And still the scruffy ponies outran them, setting an amazing pace and extracting every ounce of stamina. It was only after many miles that they were caught finally in a little hamlet and branded with the two letters they would carry for the rest of their lives.

Lucy went out with the hunters three or four times, making rapid pencil notes whenever she could and trying to remember incidents to be recorded later. Quite apart from this feat of memorising and sketching everything from horseback, the

Study for ***Colt Hunting.*** *Oil on canvas, 18in x 36in, 1897. This is probably the painting later entitled* ***Fugitives.*** *Although elements of the final composition for* ***Colt Hunting*** *appear here in embryo, the ponies were arranged later to greater effect, charging directly at the viewer.*

The Gypsy Horse Drovers. *Oil on canvas, 96in x 48in. Exhibited at the Royal Academy, 1895. Hubert Herkomer was stunned by the vigour and competence of this youthful canvas and encouraged Lucy to submit it to the Royal Academy. To Lucy's and her friends' astonishment, although it was her first submission, it was not only accepted but hung in a choice position just over 'the line'.*

size of the painting again created logistical problems for her. To be authentic she believed the picture must be completed as far as possible on site and in the open air but there was no way she could transport a canvas 10ft x 5ft into the depths of the Forest every day. Eventually she came up with a novel solution, a huge, wooden box with wide doors built to shelter the canvas in its painting position. She had this great case hauled on a cart to her chosen spot and left there under

After the round up, leading the ponies home. *Oil on canvas $6\frac{1}{4}$in x 8in.*

a tree for three months while she worked on the painting every day.

Lucy chose a full-frontal viewpoint so that the horses appear to be rushing headlong out of the picture directly at the viewer. Her determination that the painting should be as large as possible paid off too. Indeed it proved crucial to the composition, for it allowed the horses to be virtually life size and thus enhanced the impression of speed and urgency. The leaping, dark bay horse carries the massed physical energy of the galloping herd forward with him, veering to the right, while the terrified foal and the white mare, eyes dilated and nostrils flaring, vividly intensify their emotional appeal by charging straight at the onlooker. It was a cinematic idea in the days before technicolour or panavision and the impact on the picture-viewing public was tremendous.

The white horse was the key to the picture, both for Lucy and the viewers. She used her cousins' New Forest pony, Frisk, as the model, drawing and sketching her in the early summer mornings as she planned the composition out and squared the picture up. In the end Frisk was stabled at Bushey for the

Foam Horses. *Oil on canvas, 36in x 18in. Exhibited at the Royal Academy, 1896. This gave Lucy the opportunity to experiment with structures for* ***Colt Hunting*** *before embarking on the full-scale composition.*

winter until the picture was finished.

'Colt Hunting in the New Forest' created a sensation at the Royal Academy in 1897. It was, as Frith's 'Derby Day' had been in 1858, the equivalent of a television blockbuster today. It was immediately purchased for the nation by the

Preliminary study for ***Colt Hunting****.*
Oil on board, 5in x 8in, 1896.

Colt Hunting in the New Forest. *Oil on canvas, 120in x 60in. Exhibited at the Royal Academy, 1897. Lucy rode out with the hunters to capture all the images and emotions of the chase. The cinematic impact of the finished painting was tremendously enhanced by its size and launched Lucy into national prominence.*

Chantrey Bequest Fund whose collection soon after was transferred permanently to the Tate Gallery. It was rare for someone so young, particularly a woman, to be so honoured and comparisons were made between her and Lady Butler or Rosa Bonheur, then the most prominent female animal painter in Europe. *The Daily News* was lavish in its praise:

> "She gave good promise by her last year's picture, but this one comes as a surprise. It is so vigorous, and shows such knowledge of the character and of the anatomy of these half-wild animals, who come helter-skelter in a great burst upon us, their heads tossed back or thrust forward, in

every variety of action and movement. There is no feebleness or hesitation anywhere in the picture; it is all so adequate, the difficulties of foreshortening met and mastered, the landscape too so broadly treated. We must go to Rosa Bonheur to find a parallel." (1st May 1897)

The previous year, 'Summer Drought' had brought Lucy her first proper press reviews, highlighting at every turn her age and her sex. *The Times* had written, "…some of the new ladies are very much in evidence – witness Miss Kemp-Welch with her excellent group of horses in the New Forest." Elsewhere, a critic commented, "Miss Kemp-Welch, a Bushey student, has developed a talent such as is uncommon in man and quite rare in woman for animal painting."

With 'Colt Hunting' in 1897 the refrain grew louder, more incredulous – how small and feminine Lucy was, how vast and masculine the canvas. After the refreshing equality of Bushey, Lucy was impatient with gender. She made this clear when, during the clamour over 'Colt Hunting', 'Summer Drought' and two other paintings by her were selected for the Victorian Era Exhibition celebrating the Queen's Jubilee at Earl's Court. To her disgust they were put in the Women's Section, "to illustrate the progress of Woman's Art during Her Majesty's Reign." She told *The Illustrated Sporting and Dramatic News* on May 29th: "I think it is really too bad that in Art men and women should be separated. Surely Art should be considered sexless."

For all her protestations, however, her sex was relevant to the success of 'Colt Hunting in the New Forest' because, as with Anna Sewell over *Black Beauty*, the

New Forest Yearling. *Oil on canvas, 4½in x 7in.*

perspective she had taken on the hunt was unlikely to have been taken by a man. Most of Lucy's strength as a horse painter at this time derived from the perception, patience and determination she had acquired growing up with horses. Few men, by virtue of their education and status, would have had the same emotional perspective as a girl whose closest friends had been her ponies. A few years later Alfred Munnings worked on a series of horse and gypsy pictures, one of which, 'The Vagabonds', was shown at the Royal Academy in 1902. In these pictures he invariably gave as much prominence to the drovers as to their horses, so that his subject was effectively man's relationship with horses and his view was nearly always man-centred. In both 'Gypsy Horse Drovers' and 'Colt Hunting' Lucy placed rather more emphasis on the horses than the drovers, whose position in the middle to background was almost

Foals grazing in the New Forest.
Oil on canvas, 4½in x 7in.

Children of the Forest. *Oil on canvas, 18in x 24in, 1905. Lucy painted less frequently in the Forest after the turn of the century.*

incidental. Lucy's view, like Anna Sewell's, was nearly always horse-centred. Although Munnings' picture was fairly sizeable at 6ft. 6in x 4ft, it had none of the impact of Lucy's and did not sell until some time afterwards.[4]

Among other finished paintings which emerged over the summers of 1895-97 were 'Moonrise in the Forest', 'Heading off a Drive of Ponies in the New Forest', 'Fugitives' and the two pictures included with 'Summer Drought' in the Victorian Era Exhibition, 'Miss Christy's Hunters' and 'Foam Horses'. The last, shown at the Royal Academy in 1896, had been compared unfavourably by the press with 'Summer Drought', although it too had served partly as preparation for 'Colt Hunting'. Painted on the beach at Parkstone in Dorset, 'Foam Horses' was conceived as a metaphor in which white horses literally crested the waves. As a composition it allowed Lucy to explore tentatively the structural idea behind 'Colt Hunting', that the horses should leap out of the frame towards the viewer, without her having to orchestrate the finer details.

Walter Crane had employed a similar concept in 'Neptune's Horses' in 1893 and either or perhaps both his and Lucy's sea horses could have inspired Rudyard Kipling's poem 'White Horses' of 1897. In any event, Kipling's verses echoed closely the spirit of Lucy's paintings at this period. Young horses trying

4. Jean Goodman, *What A Go! The Life of Sir Alfred Munnings*, p.61.

Nightfall, the Stable Door. *Oil on canvas, 12¾in x 10¼in, 1909.*

to break free of restraints like these foam horses were a recurring theme for Lucy between 1895 and 1897. Usually depicted in herds, her ponies were displaying all the ambivalent emotions of youth, fear and delight in freedom, terror and excitement in defiance, naïvety and confidence, hesitation and recklessness. Interestingly, these pictures coincided with the period when Lucy herself was finding her feet both as an artist and as an independent woman, so that there may be parallels between the subjects she had chosen and her reaction to life at Bushey. As a graduation piece, 'Colt Hunting' was a painting most students would envy but beyond that, it possibly also represented a personal response to the experiences of her childhood and youth.

Her relationship with the New Forest was similarly evolving. Over the next few years she continued to paint there, but usually smaller family groups executed as commissions. 'Foresters' (c.1900), undertaken for a private client, and 'The Drinking Place in the Forest' (1902) for Ackermanns were among these. Likewise, 'The Forest Stream', completed between 1899-1901 and subsequently illustrated in *In The Open Country*, was possibly prompted by its purchaser, Canon Valpy of Winchester.

As for the ponies, when Frisk returned to Hampshire leaving the stable empty, Lucy found a two-year old grey colt, Stiggins, to replace her. He was nimble and intelligent like all New Forest ponies and would seek Lucy out in her studio by lifting the latch on the door and trotting in. He became a faithful helpmeet, pulling the trap loaded with painting gear round Bushey, Watford, or further afield for, now school was over, Lucy was looking beyond the Forest and her early home.

CHAPTER FOUR

"My Breaking In"

I Stood There and Listened *(Black Beauty, 1915)*

'Horses as Storytellers'

It was inevitable that Lucy's life would revolve increasingly round Bushey where Herkomer, taking her under his wing, had largely filled the void left by the loss of her parents. Moreover, she had recently bought an old house there, Kingsley, from her uncle who had acquired it while her cousin Margaret was a student. Facing the parish church on the High Street, the house had originally been the Robin Hood Inn and served Dickens as the public house, 'very cheap', where Little Nell and her grandfather stayed in *The Old Curiosity Shop*. The eighteenth century taproom was now the hall, while the lounge had been extended into the large garden. There was an orchard behind it, too, with plenty of room for the hens, stables for Stiggins and other outbuildings from which Lucy created a sizeable studio.

Fresh out of school, Lucy was lionised by the press that summer and inquisitive journalists from publications as varied as *The Illustrated Sporting and Dramatic News*, *The Ladies' Magazine*, *The Windsor Magazine* and *Black and White*, targeted Kingsley. No detail of her home was too small to be mentioned, bicycle leaning against the front door, horse brasses and roseleaf pot-pourris in the hall, carved oak furniture bearing vases of tall irises, tea-tables, french windows, Irish terrier, garden, bees,

There are direct parallels between Lucy's illustration for Chapter XXV and her Boer War painting, 'The Morning'.

In Sight! Lord Dundonald's Dash on Ladysmith. *Oil on canvas, 120in x 60in. Exhibited at the Royal Academy, 1901. Winston Churchill came to Lucy's defence in the press when she was faulted for depicting him in action here. He is third from the left.*

flowers, and pony under the apple blossom. Everything about her was news.

She was fully involved in the community, attending St James' Church, playing in the Ladies' hockey team and pursuing the latest craze for bicycling. Bushey students had a reputation for lax morals and critics complained that the school facilitated flirting. Lucy simply recalled how much she had enjoyed the many dances which to start with were very bohemian and spontaneous. Later they became quite grand and many evenings were spent preparing for them. The highlight of 1897 locally was an extravagant pageant of Kings and Queens of England, organised for the Diamond Jubilee by the Professor:

> "He himself took part and marched at the head of the pageant as the Arch Druid with all his attendant priests and druids around him, the whole scene illuminated by flaming torches. It was a memorable sight, as one episode followed another, all carefully staged in the dress of the period and accompanied by attendants with flaming torches. The scene of Queen Elizabeth I remember because I was in it. The Professor's daughter with her red hair and somewhat dominant nose made an excellent figure for the Queen and was carried shoulder high under a canopy surrounded by attendant ladies and great men of the time. The danger from fire on our march was extreme – I remember gathering up my Elizabethan skirts and jumping over the large, flaming lumps of tow and tar which fell from the torches in front. Relations and friends of some of the students who had come from London to see this sight were so impressed by the danger that they armed themselves with dripping wet blankets and pursued our procession with great perseverance and self sacrifice all the way there and back again... There were no buses and no cars in those days, to bring sightseers to this fine display of scenic art, but the whole of Bushey and Watford also turned out to look and wonder."[5]

5. Lucy Kemp-Welch papers.

The Morning. *Oil on canvas, 60in x 48in. Exhibited at the Royal Academy, 1902. Had Lucy been able to penetrate the jingoistic propaganda, she would have discovered that statistically the horse was more likely to die on the veldt than the soldier. (Present whereabouts unknown)*

Bushey graduates included a generous cross-section of future British Impressionists, among them John Arnesby Brown, his wife Mia Edwards, William Holt Yates Titcomb, Tom Mostyn, Charles Simpson, Harry Fidler, George Harcourt and Algernon Talmage. Of all Herkomer's pupils, however, the most individual, and probably most intractable, was William Nicholson. Impatient with hanging around in the Preliminary Class until he was judged mature enough to join the Life Class, he took himself off for a term or two, re-appearing in 1888. Later he chummed up with another iconoclast, Mabel Pryde, who endeared herself to Nicholson by driving a flock of geese into the classroom and eventually they married. Nicholson, with a flair for caricature which he later put to good use with his brother-in-law, James Pryde, as the Beggarstaff Brothers, was quick to penetrate Herkomer's pomposity. The antipathy was mutual. Infuriated by one of Nichlson's Whistlerian sketches, Herkomer expelled him. Nicholson for his part declared he had resigned.[6]

What Nicholson and his cohorts recognised was that for an art school, and one so close to London, Bushey was extraordinarily philistine, not surprisingly perhaps since Herkomer himself was strangely ignorant about some aspects of

6. Marguerite Steen, *William Nicholson* (1943), pp.43-44. Grant Longman however now believes that Nicholson may have spent as long as four years at Bushey.

Mangling Done Here. *Oil on canvas, 20in x 30in, 1898. Plate 17 from* In the Open Country, *the book on Lucy's work edited by Walter Shaw Sparrow in 1905.*

art. When he visited Italy at the end of the century and discovered Michelangelo, he called his students into the lecture theatre on his return to Bushey and began incredulously, "My dear boys, it has all been done! We may as well shut up shop tomorrow".[7]

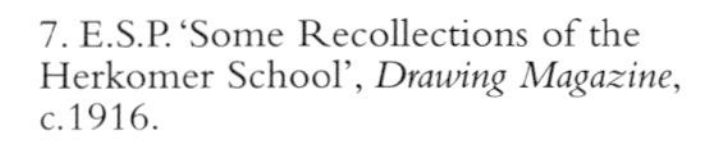

7. E.S.P. 'Some Recollections of the Herkomer School', *Drawing Magazine*, c.1916.

Bushey was exceptional among the various artists' colonies around Britain in

To Arms! Early Morning in the Duke of York's Camp before the Battle of the Roses at St Albans. *Oil on canvas, 144in x 96in. Exhibited at the Royal Academy, 1898. After this canvas failed to sell, Lucy cut it down and eventually painted* ***A Year Ago*** *over it.*

***Horses Bathing in the Sea**. Oil on canvas, 120in x 60in. Exhibited at the Royal Academy, 1900. Cavalry horses exercising in July 1899 at Parkstone, where Lucy had earlier painted **Foam Horses**.*

being focused around one dominating personality. Even Stanhope Forbes in Newlyn was a part, rather than the centre, of the colony there which had evolved originally out of a communal quest for light and the village's strategic position overlooking Mounts' Bay. Students at Bushey were forever at the mercy of Herkomer's fads, be it for enamelling, a method of underpainting, or sable brushes, and yet he despised the idea of there being a recognised 'school style'. He established rules to minimise competition between them, insisting for instance that easels should be turned to the wall at night to prevent them seeing each other's work. Yet the one trait which his pupils shared, Lucy among them, was not their style but their attitude, a pragmatic rather than a philosophical approach to art and an absolute commitment to painting from life. Formal exercises in anatomy, perspective, composition, and imagination were largely foregone at Bushey to concentrate on life drawing. The later success of many Bushey graduates, at least in Britain where John Arnesby Brown and William Nicholson both received knighthoods, derived from painting simply what was before them, England, as the English most wanted to see it, timelessly.

Sensibly, most Bushey graduates went on to broaden their studies elsewhere, often moving to Paris or Cornwall. In Lucy's case, however, after the stunning reception accorded 'Colt Hunting', further study or travel abroad seemed hardly necessary. She had already achieved success beyond her dreams or those of fellow students, and found herself the darling of the press. Her future in art, and more particularly among the Royal Academicians, seemed assured. It was a heady brew and, amidst all the gaiety, opportunities were flowing in for book illustrations and picture commissions. Unlike other pupils who had homes elsewhere and fortunes still to be made, Lucy had nothing to entice her away.

The Road to Exeter. *Oil on canvas, 54in x 30in, 1900. Begun at Bantham as a procession of Royalists following Robert Browning's Kentish Sir Byng, this painting was later reproduced as a print entitled* ***Cavaliers****.* *(Present whereabouts unknown)*

Among various books she illustrated over the next few years were E.H. Nesbit's *Pussy and Doggy Tales* for J.M. Dent and Whyte Melville's romances, *Katerfelto*, *Kate Coventry* and *Santanella* for Ward Lock. Unfortunately, this commissioned work was distracting and masked the problem she faced in establishing a distinctive, personal voice. In interviews she spoke of her determination not to get caught in a rut and acquire 'mannerisms',[8] but her difficulties were exacerbated because she had so little actual experience of art. Before arriving in Bushey, apparently, she had never seen any paintings at all except as reproductions. With scanty knowledge of the Old Masters, she had learnt little more since about Whistler or the current revolutions in French painting. Few of her contemporaries at Bushey contributed to the avant-garde New English Art Club, their artistic horizons being dominated instead by the traditional Summer Exhibition at the Royal Academy, where Herkomer was a prominent member. For all their modern social realism Herkomer's masterpieces, such as 'Hard Times' (1885) or 'On Strike' (1891), were just extensions of the story-telling pictures which had been such effective crowd-pullers at the Royal Academy earlier in Victoria's reign. Herkomer's current works, including the society portraits, were always on display when he held open house on Sunday afternoons at 'Lululand', his lavish home. Given this scenario and the expanding portfolio of illustrations, it was not surprising that Lucy adopted a narrative style for some of her next pictures.

Of these, 'To Arms! Early Morning in the Duke of York's Camp before the Battle of the Roses at St Albans' (RA 1898) was based on an historical event of local interest. Once again, it was huge, 12 feet in length, and priced at a staggering

8. *The Illustrated Sporting and Dramatic News,* 29 May, 1897.

Lucy painting ***The Road to Exeter.***

£1,000 but it remained unsold despite being sent to exhibitions in Liverpool and Bournemouth. In the end, Lucy cut the canvas in half and by 1915 had painted over it. Another attempt, 'The Road to Exeter', had an equally unenthusiastic reception and was badly hung at the New Gallery in 1903. Although completed for a D.S. Smith in December 1900, it was not paid for until January 1902 and the price, 100 guineas, was a considerable drop from the 500 guineas Lucy had received for 'Colt Hunting'. The subject had been suggested by Robert Browning's *Cavalier Tunes* and, as it was also reproduced as a print, in the long run it managed to pay its way. Nevertheless, these experiences provided a valuable lesson – the danger of depending on prevailing influences rather than personal instinct. Horses were incidental to the main subjects and both pictures, derived from solely intellectual sources, lacked the imaginative impulse which had fired 'Gypsy Horse Drovers' and 'Colt Hunting'. Lucy may have been reflecting the contemporary attitude towards horses, whose role in the economic and social structure of Britain was fundamental but largely unacknowledged. Nevertheless, it was not an attitude to which she subscribed generally nor the stance conveyed by her earlier paintings.

Fortunately, she was also exploring other avenues and some more satisfactory pictures of the period show a gradual movement towards recognising man's dependence on the horse and giving horses status. The interrelation between man and horse is the issue, for instance, in 'Horses Bathing in the Sea' (RA 1900), a development from 'Foam Horses'. It offers an advance on the freedom and restraint theme, with man forging partnerships, harnessing the forces of nature, horses and the sea. Accompanied by Stiggins, Lucy embarked on the picture during July 1899 at Parkstone, where some cavalry horses were having their annual holiday, salt water being considered good for their legs. Working on

Mixed Company at a Race Meeting. *Oil on canvas, 72in x 30in. Exhibited at the Royal Academy, 1905. This elongated canvas, begun in 1902, was the original, large version of* ***Sons of the City*** *(page 59).*

the illustrations for *Pussy and Doggy Tales* in the mornings, she spent the afternoons at the beach. Here the picture case remained perched on the sandbanks throughout August, enduring heatwave and thunderstorms before being shipped back to Bushey by train at the end of the month.

Lucy's cavalry horses, although she never advertised them as such, became suddenly topical that October with the outbreak of the Boer War. Mafeking, Ladysmith and Kimberley were cut off and besieged by Dutch settlers from the Transvaal. Following closely on Victoria's Diamond Jubilee, the War marked the zenith of imperial expansion and aroused an unprecedented wave of patriotism. National emotions ran high, fed by Robert Baden-Powell's defence of Mafeking and Winston Churchill's tales of his own adventures. It was impossible for Lucy to ignore events which provided such rousing material. Initially, perhaps, she was

trying to emulate Lady Elizabeth Butler, with whom she had been compared previously and who had become popular after the Crimean War for her military scenes. However, the succession of Boer War paintings Lucy would produce over the next three years charted her eventual retreat from story-telling.

Winston Churchill featured in her first Boer War piece, 'In Sight: Lord Dundonald's Dash on Ladysmith' (RA 1901), galloping over the last few miles of rough terrain with Lord Dundonald's troop to free Ladysmith in February 1900. Lucy had no doubt read Churchill's account of events, *London to Ladysmith via Pretoria*, written in the town immediately after the siege, but on Lord Dundonald's return to England she also approached him for his version, finding him very amiable and helpful. They met regularly over a period of months, during which she sketched him and he lent her pieces of uniform. A local artist who had served in the Cape

advised on colour and topography. An enterprising London dealer, hearing of the picture and eager to jump on the bandwagon, asked to buy it before it was finished but made a condition that it should not be shown at the Royal Academy first. Lucy refused, believing that the Royal Academy would enhance the painting's prestige and, sure enough, it was hung in a choice position wearing the discarded 'To Arms!' frame. But the attention it attracted was far from helpful. Churchill had to write to *The Times* in Lucy's defence when she was charged with inaccuracy for depicting him at Ladysmith, while other rumours spread that once again her picture had been selected by the Chantrey Bequest Trustees. Though untrue, these were possibly enough to scotch an immediate sale for, in spite of the contemporary jingoism, it was nine years before the picture finally found a home in Exeter Museum.

'In Sight' had come into being in the wake of the euphoric celebrations which took place in Bushey, and throughout Britain, on 19 May 1900, after the Relief of Mafeking. By 1901, however, after Queen Victoria's death and with casualties rising, reaction may have set in, for Lucy's next picture, 'The Morning' (RA 1902), was more contemplative and suggested a dawning awareness of the cost of war. Her working title for the composition, in which a horse keeps vigil on the veldt over a dead soldier, had been 'The Watcher', a reference presumably to the verse in Isaiah, 'The watchman said, The morning cometh and also the night.'

Although it sold immediately at the Royal Academy, it was a sentimental interpretation of events and bore no relation to the raw truth of the war for either the men or their horses. Twenty thousand soldiers died during the South African campaign but in reality more death and pain was caused by disease and ineptitude than by bullets. The toll of horses was even worse; of almost half a million horses sent out, two-thirds perished, again mostly from bad management. Regular cavalry horses were soon being supplemented with all sorts of breeds imported from all over the Empire, Europe, Russia and Argentina, to make up the incredible losses. Not only were the remounts pressed into service before they recovered from their journeys, but none of the horses had been trained for this type of guerrilla warfare, carrying heavy loads over long distances in a strange climate with inexperienced riders, reduced rations and no replacements. Saddle-sore and ill-nourished, they were vulnerable to a virulent, local, horse disease spread by gnats. The Boers' horses in contrast were generally immune to the infection and used to spending days alone on the veldt with their master carrying just a shotgun and the little they needed to survive. That a small bunch of colonial farmers could hold the mighty Empire at bay for so long was due to a great extent to the British Army's incompetent horsemastership.[9]

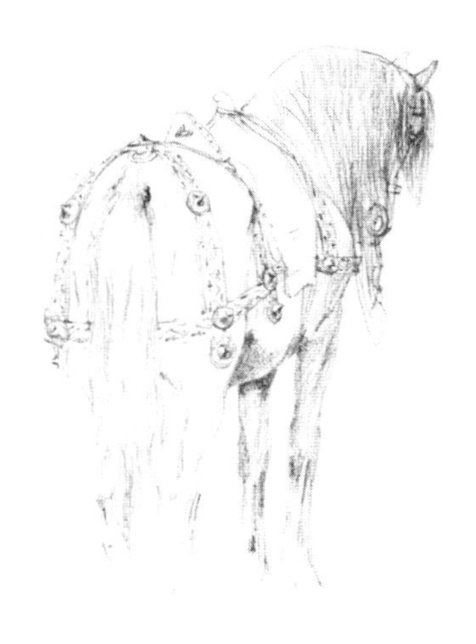

The long-suffering remounts provided Lucy with her final Boer War subject, 'Sons of the City' (RA 1903), based on sketches she made of the City of London Imperial Volunteers.[10] This was one of a number of new units raised specifically for the South

9. Charles Chevenix Trench, *A History of Horsemanship*, 1970.
10. Information from the National Army Museum.

Sons of the City. *Oil on canvas, 24in x 10in. Exhibited at the Royal Academy, 1903. A record of the City of London Imperial Volunteers who recruited men and mounts from all walks of life during the Boer War.*

African War in the outburst of patriotism and the picture was a study in the characters, not of the volunteer soldiers but of their horses. The horses, brought together from all their haphazard walks of life to be drilled into a fighting unit, were if anything more motley than their riders and a parody of the well-bred cavalry horses in 'Horses Bathing in the Sea'. The painting was commissioned in 1901 by Lord Aldenham, who lived near Bushey and was a well-known banker in the City for which he had been MP briefly between 1891 and 1892. Working at barracks in England, it would have been unlikely that Lucy knew how these horses might suffer later in the Transvaal but, as the war drew to a close in 1903, the Army set about reviewing its horsemanship. Baden Powell, hero of Mafeking, was appointed Inspector General of Cavalry and radical changes were made in the Army Manual of Horsemanship to ensure that the horses' welfare would be a priority thereafter.[11]

The war had also brought about similar changes in Lucy's perception of her priorities. Lord Aldenham thought highly of Lucy's horse paintings but disliked her figure work and 'Sons of the City' marked a transition. She had commenced one of her huge canvases for him, only to dispense with it and adapt the composition to a smaller scale. Her recipe was simple but effective, a sympathetic, even light-hearted, commentary on the disparities among the rough recruits and their unlikely vocation to the cavalry. The painting's shape emphasised her point, the long, horizontal canvas suggesting a rank in perfect military formation but the heads of the fidgety horses contradicting it. The composition had developed around a horse with a dominant blaze and the idea of creating action out of the horses' different characters was unusual, if not unique, in British horse painting at that time. For Lucy it represented progress away from self-conscious, narrative subjects and she was now refusing most offers of illustrative work. Nevertheless, she would clearly not be a painter in the tradition of Wootton, Stubbs or Ferneley either, interested in horses for their bloodlines or the sport they provided. Her interest was more subtle, more feminine, more Anna Sewell than that; it was in horses as individuals. Her insights into the horse's lot conveyed by 'Sons of the City' indicated that she had recognised at last the importance of drawing on her own instinctive horsemanship.

11. The Marquess of Anglesey, *A History of the British Cavalry, Vol. 4, 1816-1913*, 1986.

The Mangel-Wurzel Wagon. *Oil on canvas, 36in x 60in, 1902-07. A reworking of* ***The Laggard****, exhibited at the Royal Academy in 1907, from which the foreground gateposts have been removed. Decisively breaking through the horizon, the leading horse projects an heroic image of toil surmounted and this gave rise to a third, more emotive title,* ***The Crest of the Hill.***

CHAPTER FIVE

"Plain Speaking"

The Brick Cart. *(Black Beauty, 1915)*

'Horses as Labourers'

Herkomer, like Lord Aldenham, realised the path Lucy should follow long before she found it herself. In a letter dated October 1898, the Professor expressed his concern about her embarking on more narrative work after 'To Arms!':

> "I am nervous about you continuing figure work – and am absolutely certain that your success lies in animal life – preferably the horses' own life – with as much of the 'Homo' left out as possible. That has been your success and will be – your figure work is in no way up to the animal work. Don't be irritated at what I say – but I know I am right and you will see it bye and bye – but meanwhile don't risk failures. Any pure animal subject – (horses)!! And I am sure you've plenty in your head – and I hope in your heart –"

He wrote with an awareness not just of what Lucy had achieved with 'Colt Hunting', but of the hundreds of preparatory animal studies and incidental paintings which had accumulated since in her studio. He had probably laughed at 'Mangling Done Here', calves chewing the washing in the orchard at Kingsley, which was evidence not just of the livelier subjects in Lucy's head but

---

Joe Green's encounter with the angry carter in Chapter XX may have reminded Lucy of the dutiful horses who had hauled the wagon laden with mangel-wurzels in 'The Laggard'.

Ploughing on the South Coast. *Oil on canvas, 96in x 48in. Exhibited at the Royal Academy, 1902. Lucy's unsuccessful struggle to integrate the conflicting halves of this painting nevertheless helped bring greater clarity to subsequent pictures. (Present whereabouts unknown)*

of her natural vivacity, her 'heart'. For her part, she didn't screw his letter up. In fact it was one of the few letters from him which she kept, which suggests that she recognised the justice of his criticism and her own gift for painting animals. Nonetheless, exhibiting at the Royal Academy deflected her. She seemed to think that a certain gravitas was required and she was already planning a composition of which Herkomer might approve, combining animals and a timeless theme, 'Harvesters'.

Agricultural images had acquired increasing significance since the hungry Forties when the hardship and dignity of rural labourers had inspired Jean François Millet's paintings and they had percolated down the century in the social realist movement. These 'hard times' subjects, espoused in Britain by Frederick Walker and Herkomer, resounded with truth during the agricultural depression of the 1870s and were soon championed by the younger British artists then training in France. Herkomer had long held Walker up as an exemplar to his students. For their generation authenticity, relating man closely to the land he worked, went hand in hand with *plein air*-ism and by the 1890s some agricultural scenes, typically by H.H. La Thangue or George Clausen, whom Lucy greatly admired,[12] had rediscovered Millet's almost biblical dimension. By coincidence, La Thangue also submitted a harvest painting, 'Love in the Harvest Field', to the 1899 Summer Exhibition. However, any resemblance between Lucy's and La Thangue's paintings ended with the corn stooks. For Lucy was applying the social realist idiom not to people but to animals and where for her predecessors the labourers were human, for her they were going to be horses.

The outcome at this first attempt, however, was not totally satisfactory. La Thangue's couple strode across the canvas with confidence, he with a scythe over his shoulder, she carrying the gleanings, at one compositionally and tonally with the harvest field through which they moved. In comparison, the focus of Lucy's 'Harvesters' was crowded and confused, a huddle of horses and people approaching the viewer with the sun setting behind them. The horses, ambling slowly forward, and the humans, almost static, created an uneasy compromise so that the picture lacked the energy and direction which emboldened La Thangue's image.

The Magazine of Art for September 1899 re-iterated Herkomer's criticism of Lucy's recent work, the 'picture-making' in them seemed too obvious and blunted 'her own delicate insight'. However, two smaller versions of the end-

12. *Black and White Magazine*, 1 June, 1901.

Lucy in her studio with Podger, ***Harvesters*** *and* ***The Afterglow*** *are on easels behind her.*

of-the-working-day theme which she was exploring at the same time were more sincere and less obviously constructions. Their focus was simple and the results proved to be better balanced and more evocative. 'The Night Cometh', a watercolour later illustrated in *In The Open Country*, showed a gnarled ploughman and boy following their weary horses along the last furrow, while in 'The Afterglow' a ploughboy rode a team home. In both, focusing primarily on the horses, Lucy achieved a Clausenesque harmony between man, horse and environment but, although 'The Afterglow' was quick to sell at the New Gallery in March 1899, presumably she still considered the ideas too insignificant for

Harvesters. *Oil on canvas, 48in x 72in. Exhibited at the Royal Academy 1899. Although Herkomer advised Lucy not to attempt to imitate the Victorian figurative painters, she found it difficult at first to strike the right balance between men and animals in her agricultural compositions.*

Sketch for ***Timber Hauling in New Forest.*** *Oil on canvas, 12in x 24in. Lucy actually worked with teams felling and moving timber before embarking on her log-hauling studies. The extended canvas increases the tension horizontally, emphasising the powerful hauling effort required.*

the Academy.

With the Boer War intervening, it was not until 1902 that Lucy submitted another agricultural subject to the Academy. She had commenced 'Ploughing on the South Coast', another huge composition, on the cliff top at Thurlestone in Devon the previous summer and once again, both she and the painting were buffeted by August gales. In any season the weather was the major drawback to attempting large work *en plein air* in Britain but Lucy was not alone in her determination to endure for the sake of truthfulness. Stanhope Forbes suffered

Timber Hauling. *Charcoal, 14in x 22¼in. The assurance and vivacity of these charcoal strokes indicate how Lucy's confidence increased once she began to focus on working horses.*

Plough Horses. *Gouache and oil, 12in x 14¼in, 1903. This drawing and* ***Behind the Market Cart*** *were Lucy's first attempts at using Raffaelli stick paints. Their decisive marks and strong colours reflected her growing preoccupation with capturing the spirit of the horse rather than with narrative.*

equally painting 'A Fish Sale on a Cornish Beach' and contemporary wisdom doubted that a painting was genuine unless the artist had caught a cold doing it. She had roasted under an awning on the beach for the sake of 'Horses Bathing in the Sea' and even stood up to her waist in water every day for three weeks at Thurlestone in 1902 to obtain the effect she needed for 'The Incoming Tide'. There were amusing moments too, such as the occasion when some cows licked all the paint off her canvas while she was at lunch. At Kingsley her solution was a glassed extension on the grass outside the studio into which animals could be brought in poor weather, an idea she had borrowed from Herkomer who had erected a glass hut temporarily while he finished the landscape for 'Hard Times' on site.

Herkomer suggested some alterations to 'Ploughing on the South Coast' as it took final shape in February 1902. With two teams of horses working at diagonals across the picture and the foreground complicated by whirling seagulls, it still did not have quite the visual clarity of her less important sketches but its colour left behind the grim tones of Herkomer's social realism. Nor was Lucy subscribing to the concept of the labourer as a down-trodden slave, the idea conveyed by H.H. La Thangue's 'The Last Furrow' (RA 1895) in which the ploughman falls dying, hand on plough. Lucy emphasised, in contrast, not men's drudgery, but the labour of their horses, a creative gift to mankind. The animals' superiority is suggested by placing them, not under a hillside rising up oppressively behind them, as in 'The Last Furrow', but on top of the cliff or leading the ploughman downhill, in positions of potential dominance or power. The blue sea stretching beyond the horses to the horizon implies freedom too, for the wind and sea are forces of nature over which man, in spite of his intelligence, has no ultimate control. The intimation is that the horses work in productive harness with man of their own free will, or out of a sense of duty.

Lucy was working on this painting while she was also finishing 'The

***On the Downs.** Oil on canvas, 5in x 9½in, c.1913. Lucy's knack of setting white and dark horses off against each other animated even her smallest sketches.*

***In the Shadow**, 1912. The barn at Manor Farm, Cocking, where Munnings found Lucy painting one afternoon in August 1913.* *(Present whereabouts unknown)*

Morning' and 'Sons of the City', the period in which she was finding her adult voice. Soon afterwards she started 'Behind the Market Cart', comparing the heads of three horses tethered to a cart at nightfall, a condensed reworking of the idea behind 'Sons of the City'. It was a situation Lucy knew well, having brought ponies back to Kingsley this way, and she treated her subjects without sentiment, embodying the wilfulness of the grey in the toss of his head and contrasting him with his steadfast companions. It related to a series of pictures currently emerging which touched on the issues of duty and tiredness and which included, among others, 'Labourers in the Night', a pastel illustrated later in Walter Shaw Sparrow's *Women Painters of the World*. Although one horse, head lowered, strains as he pulls the last load home, his colleagues, heads high, seem bright and alert. Lucy used this balancing, 'head low-head high' formula many times to assert her subjects' dignity and resilience rather than pathos and subjugation. Not only did it provide emotional tension but it implied coincidentally an element of communication between the horses themselves, and her illustration, 'It Was Ginger', in *Black Beauty* developed out of it.

The Return from the Fields, Cocking Causeway, Sussex. *Oil on canvas, 48in x 72in. Exhibited at the Royal Academy, 1913. The deeply marked track at Cocking and the furrows beside it suggest the impact of the horses' labour on the land. The subject provides a visually and emotionally satisfying resolution of the end-of-the-day theme Lucy had explored unsuccessfully with* ***Harvesters*** *in 1899.*

By 1903 Lucy was pursuing labouring subjects actively, publicising the fundamental role horses played in contemporary society, no longer on battlefields of which she had no actual experience but, more perceptively, in the almost limitless tasks performed by every kind of fine or bedraggled horse, heavy or light, pony or shire, in the land. An incredible number of horses were employed in Britain, not just on farms but in cities and towns too. Indeed, the advent of railways and formal transport systems, rather than reducing the demand for horses, had increased it substantially. They shunted trucks and engines, delivered goods and passengers to and from termini, pulled buses and cabs, distributed food, produce and coal, hauled canal barges and manned dockyards.[13] Minding them, clearing the streets after them, provided employment for an army of men, and horse speed dictated the pace of life in town and country. The chores were never-ending and London, as Black Beauty had discovered, was full of dark, squat mews where horses who had never seen a green field lived out their days.

Wherever they lived, there was always carting to be done and in 'The Village Street' (RA 1903) Lucy again described a horse and cart making for home as night fell. She treated both man and beast with sympathy, humour even, for, although the carter seems momentarily distracted by the welcoming glow from the pub window, the horse single-mindedly carries him past, deliberately

13. *Horses: Their Role in the History of Man*, Elwyn Hartley Edwards, 1987.

The Village Street. *Oil on canvas, 72in x 48in. Exhibited at the Royal Academy, 1903. Set in Bushey on an autumn evening, Kingsley is just visible in the distance. Horse power underpinned British prosperity at the turn of the century and Lucy reflected the recurring rhythms of the horses' working day in the pattern of wheel ruts in the road.*

White Horse Pulling. *Oil on board, 10¾in x 11¼in. As a young artist Lucy also sculpted shire horses in clay but few of these models have survived.*

Sketch for ***The Passing Train.*** *Oil on canvas, 14¾in x 17¾in, 1912. Modern technology of trains and telegraph battered time-honoured, horse-drawn culture but the horses stoically prevailed. Ironically, the steam age brought more rather than less work for horses.*

ignoring the envious glances of fellow horses tethered outside. The composition is held together by a strong directional flow. The horse's head, lowered slightly, perhaps against the rain, but more especially the wheel ruts in the road, convey an impression of keen purpose and desire to return to a warm stable. The reflections of the sky in the puddles, the pointed contrasts between warm, interior and dark, exterior lights, recall Stanhope Forbes whose light effects Lucy was to echo again in the water-filled tracks of 'The Laggard'. However, where Forbes' pools and puddles were a device to bring light from the sky down into the foreground, for Lucy the depth and patina of the track itself was important as evidence of the continuous cycle of horses' labour.

The structural confidence of these recent compositions suggests that Lucy was discovering at last how to project her voice effectively. There seem to have been several versions of 'The Laggard' worked on over a period of four years from 1902 with alternative titles, 'The Mangel Wurzel Wagon' or, more significantly, 'The Crest of the Hill'. A preference for depicting single teams, ploughing, harvesting, carting, at the moment of cresting the hill or turning at the headlands, was clearly established in her pictures now. This was visually dramatic, highlighting the horses breaking across the skyline at arresting angles and at the same time, in presenting the horses literally surmounting their toil, it invested their achievements with nobility. Nonetheless, cultivating the land with horses, though it looks romantic from this distance, was a long and often wearying process. In winter the horseman had to be up before sunrise to feed and groom his team, to prepare the tackle and harness up before setting off for the fields at first light. After a gruelling day in whatever weather he had to water, stable, rub down and feed his horses before returning home. The pace was slower than in town, plodding but steady. A man and his team of two horses could plough on average an acre a day, and between them over the year, harrowing, drilling, rolling, harvesting, they managed approximately fifty acres. Farms were measured then by the number of teams employed, but good horses would lead the ploughman, drawing the furrows out straight and deep. Horsemen took immense pride in the appearance of their horses and the quality of their work, judging each others' efforts critically as they moved about the village.[14]

In Lucy's canvases the undulation of the cultivated hillside, the ridge and fall of the furrows behind the plough, the cart tracks and stooked corn, even the circling gulls, all reflect the rhythm of the horses' labour on the land. While Clausen depicted his labourers melting into their environment, Lucy depicted horses imposing pattern and order for mankind on the natural world with the farmworkers playing only auxiliary roles. The hallmark of her most successful paintings is that the animals live in harmony with their environment, either moulding it as in these agricultural scenes, embracing it as in 'Colt Hunting' and 'Foam Horses', or being enfolded by it. Although this appears fanciful, Lucy sensed it herself:

> "The English country working horse is one of these (Natural) types, in the southern counties, especially, uncultivated and beautiful. The way it fits into the landscape and is so much a part of it all. Its labour is most entrancing and subject matter for a life study."

It was not just that horses participated in nature's fecundity, tilling the soil and enriching it with their manure, but that they also mediated between man and nature. This notion adds poignancy to Lucy's timber-hauling scenes in which man trespasses on the horses' loyalty. Lucy first sketched tree-felling at Foxhills in the New Forest in 1903 but later at Ironshill and elsewhere. She spent several strenuous days working with the timber men, hooking a team of great bay horses

14. *The Farm and the Village* and *Where Beards Wag All* , George Ewart Evans, 1969 and 1970.

The Plough Team. *Oil on canvas, 12in x 16in. More often than not Lucy empowered her horses by depicting them cresting or approaching the top of hills, with men following subserviently behind.*

on to the massive boles of beech and oak and encouraging the horses to drag the timber to the immense wagons for loading. As an old lady, she claimed that she had never seen anything to equal this work for sheer violence. In 'Timber Hauling in the New Forest' (RA 1904) the vigour of the living trees, growing vertically out of the picture, complements the strength of the horses, hauling the fallen timber horizontally. The elongated canvas and the incline increase the visual tension both horizontally and diagonally, reinforcing the hauling effort and implying that the horses' great strength, life, matches the resistance of the fallen trees to death. The horses' heads are lowered not simply with the exertion but also in mourning for a companion in creation abused by mankind. This may not have been a conscious motive in her earliest timber-hauling studies with their plain speaking titles, but by 1919, after illustrating *Black Beauty*, and in the aftermath of war, titles such as 'Bier of a Monarch' and 'And His Place Shall Know Him No More' indicate that she was concerned about it.

Although felling timber is a sensitive topic nowadays, before the First World War people had little idea of how rapidly technology would threaten in turn

Turning at the Edge of the Field. *Oil on canvas, 13in x 17in, August 1913. Lucy loved silhouetting her horses on the ridge of the Downs above Cocking so that they commanded, both visually and metaphorically, an extensive panorama of the Sussex Weald.*

The Hay Wagon. *Oil on canvas, 6½in x 10½in. Discovering the Sussex Downs freed Lucy from the restraints of Bushey and contributed to an increasingly luscious use of oil paint.*

the horse, the pace of life and the very fabric of the natural world. Indeed, it was not until after the Second World War that mechanisation accelerated the decline of the working horse and changed irrevocably the speed at which life was led. The hush and tranquillity of a day spent deep in the countryside with heavy horses bears no comparison to the incessant noise and agitation of modern Britain, but when Lucy conceived 'The Passing Train' (RA 1912) the argument between tradition and progress had not acquired these connotations. She had been exploring the contrast since early 1907, when she started sketching in the goods yard at Euston Station where shire horses manoeuvred trucks more cheaply and efficiently than engines could. The parallel was straightforward. The resulting sketch, 'Titans' was intended as preparation for a larger picture, 'Power' which it seems was never finished. 'Titans' itself was sold in 1912 at the Dudley Gallery to Queen Alexandra.

In 'The Passing Train', however, interaction between the protagonists was three-way. As the horses break through the engine's smoke, they are depicted characteristically approaching the crest of the hill while the ploughman,

strategically placed behind them, is about to be engulfed in fumes. Steam was another expression of power, like the wind or sea, but man-made. Black Beauty himself had been terrified as a youngster by a train but soon learned that, although powerful, the iron horse was chained to the track laid down for it by man. 'The Passing Train' affirmed the horse's independence as, in spite of being disconcerted by the engine's noise and smoke, he could make his own tracks and break free of man at any time.

Some situations, such as timber-hauling, were compelling; they were the 'life studies' to which Lucy returned time and again. Similarly, she found horses working above the sea, or making for home at nightfall, visually and emotionally satisfying. There was an 'Abide With Me' justice in the glow of sunset balancing the horses' tired pride in a good day's work. In 1910 she spent the summer in Yorkshire, completing, among other studies 'Evening: Bolton Castle' and 'Noon: in the Dale Country', but it was the rich sequence of scenes painted in Sussex between 1912 and 1916 which marked the culmination of her pre-war farming images. Lucy usually stayed at Cocking, probably at Manor Farm, tucked beside the village church under the Downs. It was on the site of a medieval monastery and 'In The Shadow', an old grey horse gazing out of the dark barn into the sunlit yard that first summer, made the most of its ancient character. The following August Lucy invited Alfred Munnings and his wife to join her friends there. He appeared alone one Friday afternoon at tea time as she was painting in the barn and during the weekend he discovered numerous subjects there for himself.

The stream in the valley at Cocking provided the setting for 'The Glory of the Day' (RA 1914), 'The Mill Dam' and 'The Waterway' (RA 1914). The latter, with another large piece, 'The Return from the Fields' (RA 1913), proved that the concepts so hesitantly explored in 'The Harvesters' had reached maturity. Her views of horses working along the ridge of the Downs with Sussex, the sea and the sky at their feet, illustrated how far her approach had evolved in the

***The Waterway**. Oil on canvas, 72in x 90in. Exhibited at the Royal Academy, 1914. Initially entitled **The Watersplash** and then **Homecoming**, this is a counterpart to **The Return from the Fields** with the human figures almost incidental. Typically Lucy contrasted the horses' coats, gaits and head postures but this painting also shows her exploring reflections. As in Stanhope Forbes' work they bring light down from the sky into the foreground.*

decade since 'Ploughing on the South Coast'. In these sketches she luxuriated in skilfully manipulating pigment and sunlight, now in complete command not just of the animals but of her own imaginative impulse, using the light to enhance and invigorate apparently simple subjects.

Possibly the characteristics with which Lucy endowed these hard-working horses reveal something of herself as a woman. Horsemen and women are apt to be single-minded and determined, generally plain-speaking, often blunt. But as Lucy emerged into her middle years her animals reveal other qualities valuable to a woman in a man's world, discipline, integrity, dignity, duty, perhaps too an admiration for power properly directed and controlled. If that were all, however, her pictures would be sterile, but a warmth underlies this hard-won confidence and an empathy with beasts which comes only from perceptive understanding and affection. Plain-speaking they might be, but tempered like all good horses with love.

CHAPTER SIX

"A Talk in the Orchard"

My Mother and I *(Black Beauty, 1915)*

'Horses as Mothers'

The evolution in Lucy's farming subjects after 1902 reflected her increasing confidence and coincided with several years during which she appeared to become preoccupied with the mare-foal relationship. Her work had touched on this before, but always indirectly. Both 'Gypsy Horse Drovers' and 'Colt Hunting' had featured mare-foal passages, although in the former they were relatively fortuitous. In 'Colt Hunting', however, the panic reaction of mares and their foals is the main subject. The mother and foal on the left balance the tangential action of the two colts on the right. The white mare is galloping straight at the viewer and she opens the way into the picture, drawing the viewer's sympathy after her. But the composition was bound up in the urgent need to escape rather than to examine the relationship between mare and foal.

Lucy's earliest studies of mares and foals had developed in the context of the New Forest and 'Colt Hunting' but when Canon Valpy of Winchester commissioned a mare and foal painting in 1898 Lucy decided to set it in the orchard at Bushey instead. Parallels between this picture and 'Mangling Done Here' suggest that the incident with the calves probably took place while Lucy was working on Canon Valpy's picture, and both paintings revealed the light-hearted, even tender, side of

---

Lucy's sketch for Chapter I drew particularly on her experiences of painting mares and foals between 1904 and 1907.

Lucy's personality. At that stage however it seems she was too self-conscious to harness it effectively, and although mares and foals featured successively in 'The Forest Stream' (c.1899-1901), 'Foresters' (c.1900), and 'A Drinking Place in the Forest' (1902), the maternal bond was always a secondary issue.

As early as 1901, she expressed doubts about marriage and children. Painting took up most of her time and she had observed how, in spite of their education, girls who had been students with her nearly always gave up serious work once they had families. Her Irish terrier, Podger, Stiggins and a new horse, Folly, were constant companions, more amenable than any children, while in addition looking after the stables which were often occupied by visiting or borrowed horses kept her busier than many mothers. She knew she risked acquiring a reputation for rudeness, because her work was too involving for her to make formal calls, yet in spite of this Kingsley always seemed to be full of friends. She was still closely associated with Herkomer and followed the school activities,

Razina and her foal, Razzia, at the Hanstead Stud. *Oil on board, 12in x 17½in. A preparatory sketch for a formal portrait of Lady Yule's Arab mare completed in 1931.*

particularly the hockey, with interest. Meanwhile, in other social circles her success had become a two-edged sword; on one hand her renown and frank independence had made her unobtainable and on the other she did not require the status which marriage might bring. The man who won her affection would have to be intrepid and capable, as much a pioneer as she was.

The majority of her British classmates at Herkomer's school had departed by 1898 when two Americans breezed in, fresh from the Art Students' League in New York. They were Frank Richmond Kimborough, of Tennessee, and James Montgomery Flagg, later a well-known writer and illustrator. Unimpressed by Herkomer, they did little studying and instead found freelance work illustrating for journals like the *Pall Mall Magazine*. Kim developed a speciality in innovative book-cover designs using two colours on cloth. The idea caught on rapidly but, though his work was commissioned by John Lane among others, he barely scraped a living. The newcomers took digs in the High Street and for at least a year enjoyed a raffish existence, rushing to London for the music hall, socialising with society hostesses like Lady Colin Campbell, and returning to Bushey next morning still in their evening clothes.[16]

Kim was, according to Flagg, very much a man about town and quickly on as familiar terms with the county families as with the regulars in the Red Lion. Among his lady friends in Bushey was the liberated, cigarette-smoking,

16. James Montgomery Flagg, *Roses and Buckshot*, pp.59-69.

Trust: Study of a Terrier. *Oil on canvas, 20in x 24in. The title expressed not just a command to Podger but also Lucy's trust that Traddles would recover and return to his friends at Kingsley.*

American writer, Gertrude Atherton, whose frank treatment of sex in her novels had aroused criticism on both sides of the Atlantic. Lucy, petite, asthmatic and socially conventional, could hardly have been more of a contrast but, after Flagg married in 1899, she and Kim grew gradually closer. An extrovert who complemented Lucy's shyness, he was as unphased by her success and reputation as he had been by Gertrude Atherton's or Lady Colin Campbell's. By 1901 he was constantly dropping into Kingsley, inviting his own friends there, showing Lucy how to pop corn, making sweets, going skating and riding with her. Sometimes he drove Stiggins for her, on at least one occasion accompanying her to lunch at Canon Valpy's home in Winchester. They made regular visits to London, occasionally in company with Edith, to view the Academy or hear recitals and dined together afterwards, sometimes at one of his favourite haunts, the Cecil Hotel, or at Lucy's club, the Empress in Dover Street.

Kim introduced Lucy to a young Australian, Arthur Potts, whose patience as

Morning of the Year. *Oil on canvas, 28in x 36in. Exhibited at the Royal Academy, 1907. This painting was also exhibited at the Paris Salon as* ***Le Début du Printemps*** *and exemplified the maternal aspects of Lucy's character.*

a model endeared him to her forever. Throughout March 1902, Arthur sat for her almost daily while she endlessly struggled with, scratched out and revised 'The Morning' and 'Ploughing on the South Coast' in time for the Academy sending-in day at Easter. Arthur, soon nicknamed Traddles, presumably for his faithfulness, was equally popular with his fellow students and won the school sports cup in 1901. That Christmas Kim had returned to America on an extended trip but Lucy was his first call when he arrived back at Bushey in June 1902. Kingsley buzzed again with coffee parties, late night discussions, bicycling expeditions and picnics. Possibly Lucy's doubts about marriage were evaporating but her happiness was short-lived. Kim collapsed after playing badminton and died from pneumonia four days later on Christmas Eve, 1902.

Sadly, Lucy was not with him. He had been staying with mutual friends in Stanmore where she had been to see him the previous evening because he was clearly ill. The next morning she had left Bushey at seven in the morning to

spend the holiday as pre-arranged with her cousins in Parkstone. Traddles had travelled with her as far as London. She heard the dreadful news on Christmas morning and for once confided her feelings to her diary:

> "What a terrible day. Our dear Kim is dead – died last night. They were with him to the end the three. Poor Kim, so young and clever and charming. How shall we do without you. Life seems so cruel."

Kim was buried in America but a memorial service, which Flagg wanted her to attend, was held in London on New Year's Eve. Dreading the thought of it, Lucy cried off at the last minute and went to bed pleading a non-existent cold. Her last entry for 1902 concludes "Goodbye, My Friend!" Kim's death seems to have been more of a shock to Lucy than her parents' deaths had been. He was young, apparently fit, and it had happened so suddenly. According to Flagg he had 'died of popularity' and undoubtedly while he had been living in England he had burned the candle at both ends. His death placed a new emphasis for Lucy on the value of life, an urgency on its promise.

Over the next twelve months the shared grief brought her closer to Traddles

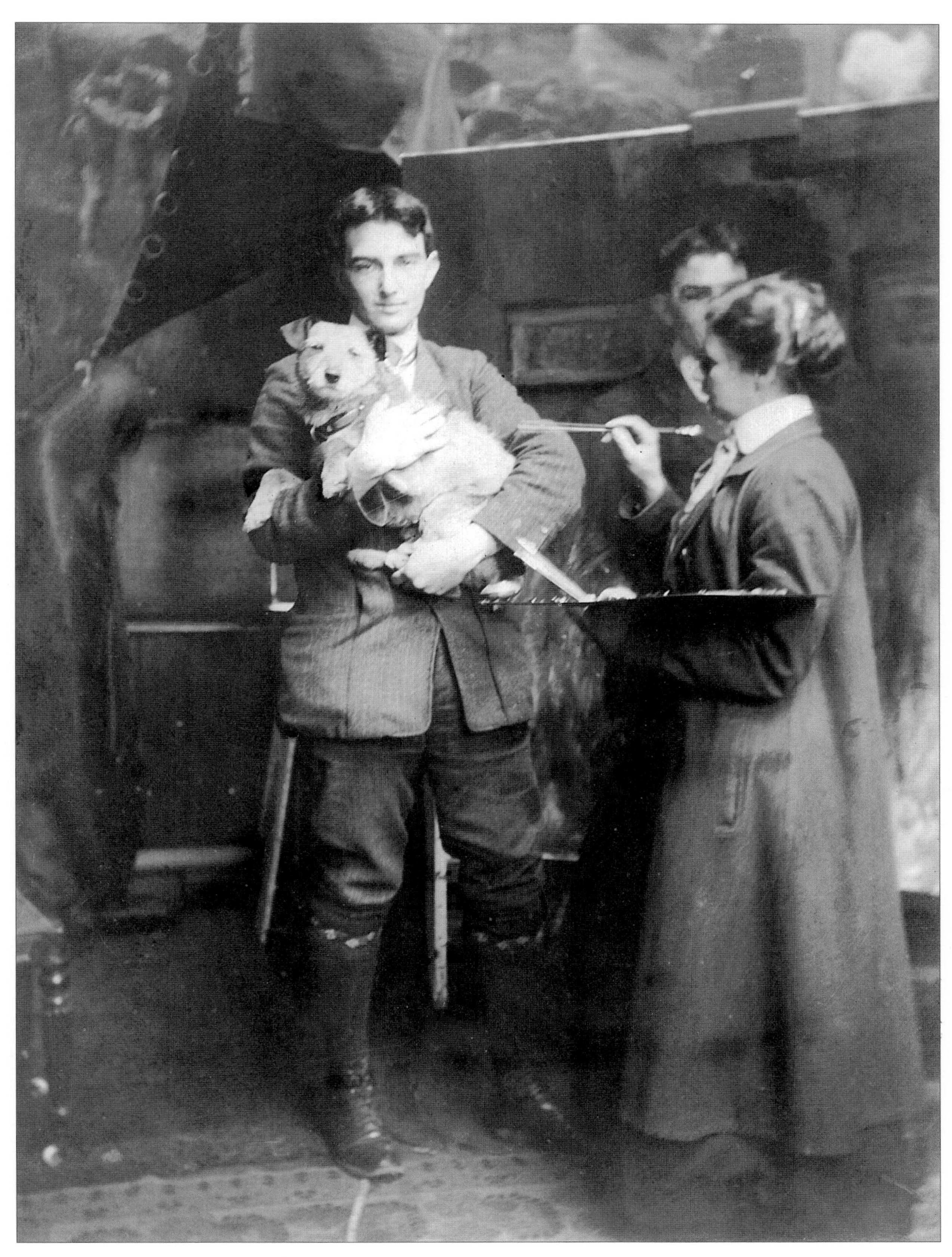

Lucy and Traddles in the studio at Kingsley.

Mare and Foal. *Pastel, 16in x 19in. This may be the pastel entitled* ***The Working Mother*** *which Lucy showed at the Pastel Society in 1925.*

although he was her junior by ten years. Accustomed to Kim's companionship and advice, she clearly missed him. Yet she was busier than she had ever been with the early months of 1903 seeing the completion of 'The Village Street', 'Behind the Market Cart' and further preparations being made for 'The Laggard'. By the summer she was travelling again in search of fresh material. She returned to the New Forest, planning the first of her timber-hauling paintings, and in early July went to Scotland where in just two days she finished 'Above the Dee'. The subjects were a Shetland mare and foal, Sheila and Pharon, and though the tenderness harked back to Canon Valpy's earlier picture Lucy was really commenting on the physical resilience of these hardy ponies on the exposed moorland. The picture was sold in August to the horses' owner, a Miss Duguid.

Lucy painted a portrait of Traddles, too, a rare concession for her and a

Sunlight Through Leaves. *Oil on canvas, 36in x 48in. Illustrated in* In The Open Country, *this was painted in the orchard at Kingsley when Traddles was dying.*

Donkey and Foal in the Heather. *Oil on canvas, 5½in x 8½in. Painting animals enabled Lucy to express feelings for which she could not find words.*

measure therefore of her fondness. When he was free he helped about the studio with Podger at his heels and became a regular supper guest. Privately and in her diary Lucy always referred to him affectionately as a boy but when at Easter 1904 he also became seriously ill with pneumonia she was thrown into a spin. For the next five months not a day passed without her visiting him in Bushey Heath hospital if not once, then twice and sometimes three times, reading him excerpts from *Punch* and taking him flowers, grapes, or peaches if they were available, which she fed to him herself as he grew perceptibly weaker. It was not difficult for her to recognise the symptoms of the pulmonary consumption from which her father had died and she wrote regularly to his mother in Australia sending reports and photographs. She had never had a young person dependent on her like this before and every day was coloured for her by the news from the hospital, his sleepless nights, the haemorrhaging, fever, hope, despair. Adding a bitter twist to the tale, Traddles' own painting 'A Maid Of Degree' was hung on the line at the Academy that summer.

Lucy now changed her working patterns and would not leave Bushey to paint elsewhere. It was as if she must give Traddles the love and attention which she had been unable to show Kim when he died. Occasionally she took Podger into the hospital to cheer Traddles up and then in June hit on the idea of painting Podger's portrait in the orchard and leaving that by Traddles' bed permanently. A walking stick lay in the grass beside the dog as if he was expecting his friends to return at any minute for their walk. For these few months the orchard was almost Lucy's only painting ground and, whether by coincidence or design, this seems to have been when and perhaps why she embarked on two of her most intimate mare and foal studies to date, 'In the Orchard' and 'What Comes?'

Both paintings feature a grey mare, perhaps the animal Lucy notes in her diary as being borrowed locally from Benskins, the brewery in Watford. 'In the Orchard', illustrated in *In The Open Country* and otherwise entitled 'Sunlight through Leaves', depicts the animals full length with the foal nuzzling the mother's side beside a tree on which the apples are just appearing. In 'What Comes?', a head and shoulders study, they look over a gate in dappled sunshine, heads and flanks together as the foal nestles closer to his parent for protection. It seemed Lucy was tentatively sounding out the implications of the mother-child bond.

By August, all hope had faded. Traddles' brother Richard arrived from Australia and on August 18th:

> "Dear old Traddles died quite quietly at six o'clock this evening. Thank God it is over for him. 'And we see him as he moved, how modest, kindly, all accomplished, wise...but through all this tract of years wearing the white flower of a blameless life.'"

The shortened quotation refers to Tennyson's Dedication to the *Idylls of the King*, which read in full gives some idea of Lucy's deep affection, maternal rather than romantic, for Traddles. Next to the entries for Kim, this ranks as the most emotional, personal comment Lucy made in her diary. After a Roman Catholic funeral, Traddles was buried in Bushey churchyard almost within sight

What Comes? *Oil on canvas, 24in x 28in. Lucy later used the image of two horses at the fence in her drawing* ***Companions*** *for* Black Beauty.

Facing page, above: ***Dwellers on the Moors.*** *Coloured chalks, 18¼in x 26in. A Dartmoor variation of the composition* ***Above the Dee****, which Lucy had painted nearly thirty years before at Balnacraig, Scotland.*

Facing page, below: ***Song Without Words****. Oil on canvas, 11in x 22in. An unusually elongated canvas highlighting the instinctive bonding which attaches the foal to his mother's side and draws him like a magnet after her. The modest size of these mare and foal canvases differentiated them from Lucy's more dramatic, public works and emphasised their intimacy.*

of Kingsley: "Very, very sad and solemn, poor dear Traddles, only 25!"

She had learnt that hard work was the only remedy for grief and she spent the whole of the next day painting the white horse before returning it to its owners. After attending the Roman Catholic church once more unusually, she then set off for a brief trip to her relatives in Parkstone.

It was to be nearly a year before she resumed the mare-foal theme, working in the orchard again with a white horse and foal. 'Song Without Words' was an extended horizontal canvas in which the horses were seen half-length, the foal running at his mother's side, his head at her shoulder. 'Morning of the Year' followed in 1906 and this was perhaps the most emotive of the whole series, the mare caressing her foal momentarily under the apple blossom. Among the alternative titles Lucy used for this picture were 'Spring Idyll' and 'Morning of Life', clues that she might have seen it as a metaphor for rebirth. As a practising Christian it would have been natural for her to assuage her feelings of waste and loss by expressing her belief in resurrection.

The dating and reiteration of similar motifs throughout this series seem to confirm this. Lucy made numerous revisions as her feelings gradually changed. 'What Comes?' remained unfinished until 1907 when 'Song Without Words' was also altered, or, as Lucy noted, 'improved'. 'Morning of Life' was completed that year, too, in time for the Royal Academy and was selected for the Paris Salon in 1908. By then she had apparently come to terms with the deaths of her friends and had even consigned 'Trust', the portrait of Podger which she had given to Traddles, to an exhibition at the Royal Society of British Artists. However, although she touched on the image of mare and foal frequently after the First World War, it was generally for commissions and never again with the same personal indulgence and intensity which she had displayed after Traddles' death.

She acknowledged now that she would never marry and it was through bereavement rather than motherhood that she had acquired the tenderness which allied so well with her other strengths. Just as these early mare and foal paintings were guarded from mawkishness by an underlying restraint, so her labouring pictures were now charged with an underlying warmth. Possibly her attachment to Kim had taught her not to be frightened of her emotions. Flagg testified how attractive Kim was and to someone from Lucy's inhibited background he must have seemed tremendously refreshing, cosmopolitan and romantic, his energy fatefully concealing how similar his constitution was to her father's. In any event, their relationship marked her coming of age. Relaxed and uninhibited with Kim, she was no longer self-conscious about looking into her heart as Herkomer had suggested and her paintings silently celebrated it.

Unfortunately, other events at this time were to have a less constructive outcome. During the crisis of Traddles' tuberculosis, serious problems had arisen at Herkomer's school. Lucy was too distracted to play an active part until matters reached a head and criticism of the school began to appear in the press.

Companions. *Pen and ink, 4⅛in x 6in, illustration from* Black Beauty. *This drawing appeared twice in* Black Beauty, *first when as a colt Black Beauty made friends with Ginger at Birtwick Park, and then later at Earlshall, their last home together.*

On 24 May, 1904 Herkomer resigned as president and its closure seemed imminent. At this point Lucy intervened, perhaps out of gratitude to the Professor who had done so much to support her, and she started negotiations to buy the school. It was a bad time emotionally for her to take such an important, personal decision but she felt she must protect Herkomer from humiliation. She was to live with the consequences of this ill-judged step for the next twenty years. Having foregone motherhood for her painting, she hampered herself with a school instead.

The Riders. *Oil on canvas, 84in x 96in. Exhibited at the Royal Academy, 1911. Black Prince and his lady rider make a formidable partnership in Lucy's most overtly 'feminist' picture. In the yin-yang of contrasts between horses and riders even the measures of the horses' strides counterbalance each other.*

CHAPTER SEVEN

"A Strike for Liberty"

Now Auster do Your Best *(Black Beauty, 1915)*

'Horses as Emancipators'

Taking over Herkomer's school, however ill-suited Lucy was to running it, was a public declaration of self-confidence. It represented a major advance for women, too. Although Louisa Gann and Fanny McIan had headed the Female Art School earlier, and Louise Jopling had established a school for women artists at her home in Logan Place, Lucy was the first female principal of an art school with pupils of both sexes in Britain. Women were still not accepted as teachers in the Royal Academy Schools, nor as yet at The Slade, although since its opening in 1871 the latter had attracted a high proportion of women as students.[17]

The century had dawned full of promise for Lucy with her most recent painting, 'Horses Bathing in the Sea', enthusiastically received by the Royal Academicians in April 1900. Though she was only thirty, Herkomer took this chance to propose her for election and Lucy was stunned to realise how well supported was her candidacy. As the excitement mounted she went for an outing with friends to Chenies, she driving Folly and Kim Stiggins. On their return to Bushey they were greeted by Herkomer's report from the hanging committee, an exciting end to a wonderful day. Lucy was on top of the world and still the praise mounted:

"Thursday 26th April: Picture well hung. Professor delighted, says best of

17. For further details of women's art education, see Pamela Gerrish Nunn, *Victorian Women Artists*, 1987 and Paula Gillett, *The Victorian Painter's World*, 1990.

The landscape through which Black Beauty, Auster, raced in Chapter XXIV to fetch the doctor was based on the Yorkshire moors where Lucy had painted 'The Riders' in 1910.

all outside work! Incredible!
Friday 27th April: Professor gives wondrous accounts of the way the RA's received picture.
Monday 30th April: Varnishing Day. Picture looking very well. RA's very kind and saying works of genius etc. Davis RA especially, and Seymour Lucas. Val Prinsep said he had seconded my name for the Academy. All very enthusiastic. It is overwhelming."

If Lucy was elated, others were alarmed. There had been only two female members of the Royal Academy since its foundation in 1769 when Angelica Kauffmann and Mary Moser had been admitted to partial membership. More recently, in 1879, Lady Butler had been proposed but was beaten in the ballot, ironically by Herkomer himself, and then by only two votes. That he was a foreigner was evidently less frightening to the Academy diehards than that she was female, and for his part Herkomer had been grudging about having so nearly lost to a woman. But the climate had changed in the intervening years and women were much more in evidence in public life, adding to Lucy's chances of winning.

Nevertheless, at the eleventh hour the old guard rallied and to Bushey's disappointment, Henry Scott Tuke and Joseph Farquharson were admitted instead. W.P. Frith, foremost among the reactionaries, pausing nevertheless to admire one of Lucy's paintings, explained that they had had 'a narrow squeak' once before with a woman, Lady Butler, and they couldn't risk it happening again. It looked as if Lucy had been rejected solely because she was female, but

The Incoming Tide. *Oil on canvas, 38in x 48in. Exhibited at the Royal Academy, 1903. Lucy stood up to her waist in water under the cliffs at Thurlestone everyday for three weeks to tackle this subject.*

the painters elected were also older and more experienced than she, Tuke being forty-eight and Farquharson fifty-four. Lucy was young for membership and, as is now evident, still feeling her way in her career.

Moreover, being philosophical, it would surely be only a matter of time before justice prevailed and events in the years immediately following hastened to confirm this. In 1901, 'In Sight' also met with acclaim when it was hung in the place of honour. The following year both 'Ploughing on the South Coast' and 'The Morning' were hung on the line and drew praise from Quiller Orchardson. This placing of Lucy's pictures at the Academy was in itself significant. They were nearly always 'on the line' which, at eye-level, was the best space on the wall and usually reserved for the Academicians themselves. Meanwhile, plaudits were arriving from other quarters too and in January 1902 the Royal Society of British Artists invited her to stand for election there. Her immediate acceptance as one of their first lady members endorsed the public image of a woman moving with growing assurance in a man's world.

This was a far cry from the timid girl who had stepped into Herkomer's school

Study of Ducks Bathing in a Pond. *Oil on canvas, 8½in x 10½in. This small oil sketch was illustrated in* In the Open Country *in 1905.*

only a decade before. Numerous factors had contributed to the transformation, Herkomer's encouragement, her own hard work and determination, the astonishing artistic achievements of those first few years, and last but probably not least her relationship with Kim. Along with affection and humour, he and his friends had brought Lucy New World objectivity too, quickly discerning, like William Nicholson, the flaws in Herkomer's façade. They leavened the predominantly female atmosphere of Kingsley, where they made irreverent and pointed jibes at her most lauded paintings, particularly 'In Sight'. Cartoons lampooning Lucy and Dundonald suggest that Kim may well have provided the spur which Lucy had needed to make a break for it. He was at her side on Varnishing Day 1901 to hear the chorus of approval and carried her off to lunch afterwards at the Cecil Hotel. He was clearly both a talented designer and a capable horseman. Was it merely coincidence that, as they grew closer, Lucy's vision became increasingly focused and perceptive and she rediscovered at last the vital 'impulse to paint' of which she had lost sight after 'Colt Hunting'?

Although Lucy explained this phrase to Edward Seago in 1932 in terms of

***The Orchard Gate.** Watercolour, 9¼in x 12in, c.1909. A preparatory study for **Young April,** this watercolour was bought by a young Canadian officer, Philip Dennison, after World War I.*

lighting, mass and design, the words she used suggest she actually meant something more fundamental, the feelings which underlay his response to a scene:

> "You have been so carried away by the passing show that you have forgotten what made you feel the impulse to paint it – not the facts – not the commonplaces of clowns and dwarfs and Red Indians etc. They go for nothing. But a fine effect of light on a massive design with all the component parts and little masses lost or half seen in the group mass; everything secondary to some big idea of mass or colour or light."[18]

It was because Seago had lost sight of his feelings that the circus painting he had submitted to the Society of Animal Painters had been rejected and, although she may never have recognised it, this was the reason why Lucy had lost her way too after 'Colt Hunting.' Too many facts encumbered the feelings.

Retrieving the 'impulse to paint' dramatically simplified Lucy's paintings both thematically and visually. 'An Idle Day: Tommy and Steamer', begun just after 'Sons of the City' was despatched in 1902, heralded the new sureness of touch. Mr Spicer, a neighbour, commissioned a portrait of his horses and within two

18. Jean Goodman, *Edward Seago, The Other Side of the Canvas*, 1978.

Study for ***Market Night****. Charcoal, 22½in x 19¼in. Horses fighting against restraint and domination were a recurring theme in Lucy's painting and had found an echo in Ginger's story. Lucy later cut* ***Market Night*** *itself up.*

days Tommy and Steamer were grazing in Lucy's orchard. Next morning, Wednesday 23 April, she set to work, concentrating on the painting almost exclusively until Saturday when Mr Spicer came over in a bitterly cold wind to check on its progress. He returned the following week with his son but, after the initial burst of activity, the new painting had to be fitted round other commitments, including preparations for the Coronation and a tableau in the village. Nonetheless, by 5 July, after Kim's return from America, it was virtually finished. There were no distractions from the main design now; the 'fine effect of light' fell on the horses themselves with Podger's yapping a succinct counterbalance to their easy canter round the orchard.

'An Idle Day' was an unencumbered celebration of these happy times at Kingsley. Suddenly Lucy's work had gained a new dynamic. She dispensed with obvious narrative and from now on selected her material more rigorously. She placed the subject more decisively and used light to give it unity, drive and purpose. That was the summer at Thurlestone when she embarked on 'The Incoming Tide', a composition virtually abstracted from 'Ploughing on the

***Chestnut horse exercising**, c.1902. Oil on canvas, 10in x 9in. Tommy and Steamer rapidly settled into the regime at Kingsley which revolved around animals and friends.*

The Joy of Life. *Oil on canvas, 96in x 144in. Exhibited at the Royal Academy, 1906. Although Lucy qualified this picture with a quote from* Henry V, *the title itself may have been borrowed from Browning's* Saul *in which David sings of* 'the wild joys of living! the leaping from rock to rock.'

Sketch for ***The Joy of Life****. Oil on panel, 9½in x 14in, October 1905. At some point in the planning of the finished picture the action was moved from right to left.*

For Life. *Oil on canvas, 60in x 120in. Exhibited at the Royal Academy, 1908. Lucy explained this painting in her Dudley Gallery catalogue: 'With the Devon and Somerset Hounds the hunted stag frequently endeavours to elude the pursuit by running with a herd of wild ponies. As the hounds come nearer, however, he leaves this shelter and dashes again into the open.'*

If Only I Could Get Him Off, *illustration from* Black Beauty. *In Chapter VII Ginger described for Black Beauty the cruelty she suffered when Samson Ryder tried to break her in and she longed for gentleness and understanding, the more intuitive, feminine approach to horses which Lucy favoured.*

*Study for **Sport of Imperial Rome**. Charcoal, 28in x 19in, 1931-32. Lucy's subjects were usually depicted from the horses' rather than man's point of view. Tacitly they implied that man's attempts to master rather than partner his horses were vainglorious.*

South Coast' of the previous year. Lucy took the birds which had complicated 'Ploughing' and let them flock and mewl round the base of the cliffs in a canvas of their own. In 1905 it was chosen by the art critic Walter Shaw Sparrow as one of the illustrations for the book he was editing on Lucy's work, *In The Open Country*. An appreciation in this by Edward Strange paid tribute to Lucy's role as a pioneer among British women artists and sought to dispel the prejudice her work encountered because of her sex. Meanwhile, Herkomer in his foreword commented how remarkable it was that after twenty-one years of giving men and women equal opportunities in his school, a woman was now publicly recognised as his most successful pupil.

Perhaps coming to terms with the deaths of her two closest male friends helped rationalise Lucy's attitude to petty sexual politics. In any event, by the time the book was published she was well into her stride, typically disregarding gender. Her first one-man show had opened at the Fine Art Society in Bond Street on 19 May. The bereavements, rather than destabilising her, seemed to be concentrating her efforts. Not only had they given rise to the series of thoughtful mare and foal studies but more defiantly they were also inspiring her to re-interpret the ideas of liberty and freedom expressed in 'Gypsy Horse Drovers' and 'Colt Hunting'. Dealing in the elemental terms of life and death rather than in mere youth, made issues of gender irrelevant. The very title she chose for the first of these new pictures, 'The Joy of Life' (RA 1906) is a contradiction of death, a challenge. The subtitle, from Shakespeare's *Henry V*, 'In the very May morn of his youth, Ripe for exploits and mighty enterprises',

Mare and Foal on the Moors. *Oil on canvas, 8in x 10in, 1908. Exmoor ponies grazing near Simonsbath when Lucy was painting* ***Reprieve.***

An Idle Day, Tommy and Steamer. *Oil on canvas. 30in x 50in, 1902. Mr. Spicer's horses cantering round the orchard at Kingsley heralded a new dynamic in Lucy's painting.*

came from the speech in which Ely urges the King to renew the feats of their valiant ancestors. With no evidence of a hunt, the painting expresses purely the horses' exultation in being alive. As in 'Colt Hunting' there is a real feeling that in the momentum the stampede will burst out of the massive canvas. The sense of their dominance and power is intensified by their being on top of rising ground, rearing up and moving down aslant the canvas as a body.

She returned to the theme again in 'For Life' (RA 1908) which featured a stag hunt on Exmoor. She scouted out the landscape around Simonsbath in 1907, visiting the Doone Valley and Watersmeet, and riding over to meets at Cloutsam

Farmyard Gate. *Watercolour, 11in x 14in. Probably painted in the Dales in 1910.*

Lucy Kemp-Welch on Black Prince appearing in Herkomer's film, A Highwayman's Honour, *1914.*

and Bridgeworthy. She was helped in her research by Lord and Lady Fortescue whose home, Castle Hill at Filleigh, was on the edge of the moor. They took Lucy up to Prayway Head where they had some ponies and it was here that Lucy asked the Hunt to erect her picture case. The Fortescues also arranged for the staghounds and a dead stag to be taken back to Castle Hill after one of the meets for Lucy to sketch them in comfort. She noted how "with the Somerset and Devon Hounds the hunted stag frequently endeavours to elude pursuit by running with a herd of wild ponies. As the hounds come nearer, however, he leaves this shelter and dashes again into the open." In contrast to 'Gypsy Horse Drovers' and 'Colt Hunting', the dogs and hunters are only specks on a distant hill. The stag and horses, breasting the hill, though galloping for their lives, have a formidable lead and in evading capture are cheating death.

Stag's Head. *Oil on canvas, 13in x 11in, 1908. Painted on Exmoor. Lucy sympathised characteristically with the huntsmen's quarry, admiring the courage of those who struck out for freedom.*

Head of a Grey Arab*. Watercolour, 12in x 16in, 1905. Lucy inscribed this watercolour a second time when she gave it away in July 1906. It had previously appeared in* In the Open Country.

Initially the Hunt had lent Lucy a cob on which to explore Exmoor but one outing was sufficient to prove him "dreadful, very quiet". Another pony was offered with an equally unhelpful result, "very lively". Finally Lucy boxed her own horses, Folly and the new stable mate, Black Prince, down by train and they arrived at South Molton towards the end of August. Black Prince had been at Bushey a little under a year by this time but he was already closely identified with Lucy and though she never owned him they were destined to play important parts in each other's lives. He would eventually be immortalised as Black Beauty, the real horse virtually indistinguishable from the fictional.

Black Prince, an intelligent, handsome, black charger of about seventeen hands, actually belonged to Robert Baden-Powell and was one of two horses presented to him after Mafeking by the people of Australia through a fund got up by a Melbourne newspaper.[19] Both horses had been shipped to Baden-Powell in South Africa and the second, Orara, would die in service during the First World War.[20] For his part, Black Prince did not take naturally to the parade ground, jibbing and rearing at gunfire so that, by the time he came to Lucy, Baden-Powell had not ridden him on parade for three years and had lent him temporarily to the artist, Emil Fuchs. Meanwhile, Baden-Powell was considering either selling or putting Black Prince down when as a last resort he

19. Letter from Baden-Powell to Lucy Kemp-Welch, 7 March, 1908.

20. Information from the Hon. Mrs Betty Clay and Tim Jeal.

The Kemp-Welch School headpiece.

offered him to Lucy as a model for her school and she accepted with alacrity.

Lucy had been introduced to Baden-Powell at the Royal Academy on New Year's Eve 1904 and he visited the school in 1905. Not only did they have friends in common, Lord and Lady Lockwood, but Baden-Powell was also a keen amateur artist; an exhibition of sketches, illustrating his years in South Africa, being held in London in 1907. He explained to Lucy that Black Prince was not a nice lady's horse, indeed he had never been ridden by a lady before, but he hoped his behaviour might have improved with age. Between the lines the assumption was that if anyone could master him, man or woman, it would be Lucy. It was the sort of task she relished. Moreover, Black Prince arrived at Bushey in the aftermath of her grief for Kim and Traddles. Lucy committed herself to exercising and schooling Black Prince regularly, yet after several years there were still occasions when he "behaved disgracefully". Once he objected to the armour she was wearing for a theatrical performance with him, forcing her to change costumes at the last minute. On Exmoor in 1908 he escaped and ran off with the wild ponies so that Lucy had to treck back and fetch Folly in order to recapture him. Her students complained that he was a fidgety model but, miraculously, whenever Lucy appeared in the studio he would pose perfectly and then she berated them for careless work. Nevertheless, by the time Baden-Powell's children learnt to ride on him in the early Twenties, he was almost tame. They recalled climbing on his neck when he was cropping the grass and sliding down gently on to his back as he raised his head.[21]

Baden-Powell had much admired 'For Life' when he saw it at the Academy in June 1908 and that summer at Simonsbath Lucy embarked on a sequel, 'Reprieve', showing a deer hidden from his pursuers by the mist. Reminiscent of Landseer's 'Monarch of the Glen', it lacked Lucy's usual vitality and was rejected by the Royal Academy in 1909. She would have done better submitting 'Young April' (RA 1910), a much more spirited painting, but had been dissuaded from doing so by Herkomer who felt it was unfinished. Nonetheless, 'Young April' spoke from the heart, imaginatively uniting various themes which had preoccupied Lucy since 1895. The subtitle drew upon Shakespeare's sonnet, 'From you have I been absent in the spring, When proud pied April … Hath put a spirit of youth in everything.' Although Black Prince did not model for the painting – Lucy borrowed a grey mare from Sears' farm – his schooling may have contributed to its conception, for the subject is a young girl tempering a skittish horse and its bewildered foal by tenderness and intuition rather than

21. The Hon. Mrs Betty Clay.

Watercolour sketch for ***The Riders****. 8½in x 11½in. In the early stages of composing* ***The Riders*** *Lucy had changed the man's horse from dark to white, greatly improving the balance of the finished picture.*

confrontation. Maybe it sprang out of Lucy's girlhood relationship with horses, but it also represented a synthesis of more recent preoccupations, youth and freedom, escape and control, mare and foal, love, loss and rebirth. Indeed 'Young April' brought the mare and foal studies to a robust climax, accentuating the potentially creative partnership women have with nature, and by extension therefore with society. Although Lucy was no suffragette, the girl, in seeking to conciliate rather than dominate as a man might, presents a specifically feminine viewpoint.

This idea was pursued with greater vehemence in 'The Riders' (RA 1911), probably the most overtly feminist of all Lucy's pictures, painted at Carperby in Yorkshire in 1910. Largely due to Lucy's commitments at the school, 'Young April' had been painted, like the previous mare and foal studies, in the orchard at Bushey. Increasingly, however, she preferred to get away from Bushey whenever she could, finding moorlands like Exmoor, where she could shed her responsibilities completely for a couple of months in the summer, especially seductive. It was Baden-Powell, while staying at Richmond Castle in 1908, who encouraged her to visit Yorkshire to see the particular local breed of heavy horse, probably the Dales ponies rather than Cleveland Bays. Although he recommended the wolds between Malton and Beverley, Lucy chose instead Aysgarth, Swaledale and the valley of the River Ure, now 'James Herriot country'.[22]

Some smaller farming pictures resulted from this visit and once again Lucy was welcomed and entertained by the local landowner, Lord Bolton, but for her largest composition the picture case was set up athwart the moors in full force of the prevailing wind with only a dry-stone wall for protection. On one occasion the gusts were so strong that she had to take the rope off Black Prince

22. Baden-Powell correspondence, Boy Scouts Association.

Waiting in the Shade. *Oil on canvas, 12¾in x 19in. The richness of oil paint helps to orchestrate this contrast between the dark, glossy flanks of the Exmoor ponies and the glare of the midday sun.*

Ponies on the Moor. *Oil on canvas, 4¾in x 8¾in, c.1908. Wild ponies breaking free always had a particular attraction for Lucy and immediate, small, oil impressions such as this were the snapshots from which she built her huge, finished compositions.*

On the River Barle, Exmoor. *Watercolour, 7in x 11in, 1908. Probably a study for the small oil painting,* ***Sapphire and Gold,*** *this watercolour was sold at the RCA in 1925 for 12 guineas.*

to tie the case down and on several days grouse-shooting kept her off the hill. Nevertheless, the panorama was literally breathtaking and Black Prince, now nicknamed 'BP' after his master, came into his own. Indeed 'The Riders', derived from Browning's poem 'The Last Ride Together', capitalised on Black Prince's maverick character. The picture was not free of the shades of Kim and Traddles either. A Miss McCabe, later Mrs Colpitts, modelled for the woman while Arthur Curwen, Edith's constant companion and an old friend of

Ben – A Study of a Lurcher. *Oil on canvas, 28in x 36in. Lucy painted this lurcher at the request of his owner, Lady Muriel Herbert.*

On the Purbeck Hills. *Oil on canvas, 9½in x 13½in. Philip Dennison bought this painting from Lucy in 1921, writing from Canada with the description of a similar painting he had once admired in her studio.*

The Salmon Pool. *Watercolour, 14in x 20in. Exhibited at the Royal Academy in 1905. Illustrated in* In the Open Country *(pl.8) where it was entitled* ***Sheep by the Sea.*** *Lucy painted this watercolour at Bantham in 1902.*

Traddles, sat for the man. Sadly, Arthur was also suffering from tuberculosis and died some years later. As if to emphasise her femininity, the lady rides side-saddle as Lucy had done herself until 1907 when she had one of the new habits made. Amusingly, riding astride made her feel "very unsafe and wobbly" at first.

In Browning's monologue, the suitor pleads for a last ride with the lady who has rejected him. While they gallop across country he wonders whether heaven will simply be this, the crowning moment of his youth, caught in eternity before it can fade: 'What if we still ride on we two, With life forever old yet new'. Lucy replies for Browning's silent woman, the yin-yang of the picture's contrasts and ironic reversals dramatically clarifying the reasons for her refusal: woman on dark stallion, man on white mare; she self-sufficient, perceptive, free, he suppliant, obtuse, hampered; her horse powerful but controlled, his edgy, perplexed; he pursuing an illusion, she confronting reality. Browning's poem perhaps awoke memories of happier rides with Kim, but the general implication would seem to be that in any relationship with a man the woman is looking for the blend of mutual respect and understanding which she achieves with the horse, neither of them compromising the other's independence. In the absence of that she remains unmoved. At a personal level therefore it appears highly charged, a statement both of faith and of farewell.

More generally, it is tempting to interpret 'The Riders' as a commentary on the position of women before the First World War. The pressure for woman's suffrage had been building up since the turn of the century but the militant suffragettes, as opposed to the less aggressive suffragists, had polarised the debate and done much to hamper progress. Feminists, of whom Gertrude Atherton was one, were quite at home in Bushey with its artistic and intellectual freedom but although she had several friends in Bushey who actively supported the suffrage campaigns, the Woodward sisters and Elizabeth Gulland for instance, Lucy herself seems not to have taken a political stand.[23] She was also acquainted with Mrs Humphrey Ward, the novelist and leader of an anti-suffrage league and when Emily Davison had thrown herself under the King's horse at the Derby in 1913, Lucy's reaction was of equal concern for the horse and jockey. Certainly 'The Riders' was topical but it appears to have reflected a personal rather than political position with Lucy, impatient with the petty encumbrances of gender and the school, asserting that independence was achieved by using one's own especial talents constructively.

Lucy put this theory into practice in 1913, when she instigated the formation of the Society of Animal Painters. She had recently enjoyed a second one-man show at the Dudley Galleries in 1912 attended by Queen Alexandra but, in spite of her own success, one of the problems most women painters encountered was finding such forums where their work could be shown and valued as equal to men's, and not treated as amateur dabble. She had exhibited very briefly with the Society of Women Artists but found that by its very nature it isolated rather than integrated women into the art market mainstream. Lucy's

23. Anne Leslie, Bushey Museum Trust.

idea of a society unified by a common subject rather than by gender seemed infinitely preferable. Having sounded it out with Robert Morley, former secretary of the Royal Society of British Artists, she approached among others Alfred Munnings, Lionel Edwards, Arnesby Brown, Briton Rivière, George Pirie, Frank Calderon, H.W.B. Davis, Herbert Dicksee, Arthur Wardle and John Charles Dollman to see if they would be interested. Munnings was very positive and by March 1913 they were making plans. By July a room had been hired at the Leicester Galleries for the inaugural exhibition and in late October Lucy was elected President. This gesture, the public acknowledgement of her ability by her peers, meant a great deal to Lucy and she had earned it. When the show opened on 6 January 1914, reviewers remarked that her paintings were the strongest there.

An invitation to Buckingham Palace for the Royal Garden Party, coinciding with her birthday in 1908 and the start of her fortieth year, had been yet another cause for celebration. Lucy was at the height of her powers and she had no need, or time, to be a suffragette. In that period leading up to the First World War, it seemed that her success as an artist and her life with horses had already effectively emancipated her. She had bought her own home, had run her own school, earned and invested her own money, was treated as an equal by generals,

Sunlight and Shadow, Hyde Park. *Oil on canvas, 24in x 30in. Exhibited at the first Society of Animal Painters' show in 1914, where Lucy's work was judged as stronger than her male contemporaries', this painting was described by* The Studio Magazine *as 'a clever sketch' and by* The Illustrated London News *as 'a spirited picture'. Rotten Row was an unusually frivolous painting ground for her, and somewhat diluted the urgency conveyed by* ***The Riders****, but within months foreign military attachés such as this one would have had other, more pressing concerns.*

businessmen and horse dealers, was even recognised as a leader and spokesman by fellow artists. Only one honour had so far eluded her, election to the Royal Academy. It is difficult to appreciate the awe in which Royal Academicians were held by the general public in those days, the prestige and authority membership gave to artists. Lucy had stood back as the first of Herkomer's students, Arnesby Brown, was elected ARA in 1903. Richly though she now deserved these laurels herself, ironically she may have been cheated of them in the end by the suffragettes themselves. Their intensified campaign from 1906 provoked a backlash within the establishment. Whether Lucy accepted it or not, her sex had always been an issue and was going to remain so.

CHAPTER EIGHT

"A Stormy Day"

Fire! *(Black Beauty, 1915)*

'Horses as Heroes'

The declaration of War on 4 August 1914 found Lucy at Cocking. Within twenty-four hours, rumours had spread that the Downs were to be entrenched and all horses commandeered. When reports of Remount Purchasing Officers in the area reached her on 25 August, she prayed fervently that Black Prince would be too old and luckily he was passed over. It was a relief too that Herkomer's death on 31 March had saved her old Professor and Bushey from a conflict of loyalties. In Germany his love of motor racing had led to his founding the Herkomerkonkurrenz, now the German Grand Prix, while in Bushey he had also done much to support the local community, raising funds through his theatricals to finance the village nurse and encouraging employment through his ventures into printing and craft work. Only a few months earlier, in February 1914, Lucy and Black Prince had been among many given their film debut as extras for his production, 'A Highwayman's Honour', set in the grounds of Bushey Hall. Yet, although he had been decorated by the Kaiser in 1899 and knighted by Edward VII in 1907, in neither Germany nor England would he have been fully accepted now.

This was the first illustration Lucy tackled, one of only two oils on canvas in the project, for J.M. Dent in February 1915. With the horses shying but being driven regardless through the smoke and tumult, it predicted the composition of 'Forward the Guns!' in 1916.

Big Guns up to the Front. *Oil on canvas, 78in x 150in. Exhibited at the Royal Academy, 1918. The success of* ***Forward the Guns*** *nationally encouraged Lucy to embark on a larger picture highlighting the contribution not of artillery horses but of the less romantic heavy horses at the Front.*

Relations between Britain and Germany had been deteriorating over years but the social changes the War brought about, not least in public attitudes to women, were rapid and decisive. Often, when working class men joined up, their wives took on their jobs to maintain the family income and keep their positions open for when they returned. This was the case not only in transport and factories but for the self-employed trades too, like window-cleaning, bill posting, chimney sweeping, coopering and even blacksmithing, which had hitherto been regarded as male preserves. Mrs Pankhurst pledged the support of the Women's Social and Political Union, the suffragettes, to the war effort and middle or upper class women of all political persuasions were united in giving their services voluntarily to the cause. In late August and September 1914, for instance, Lucy was busy making shirts for Queen Mary's Needlework Guild, one of the first organisations to distribute necessities to servicemen and their dependents.

Working on the family farm or nursing were already acceptable occupations for women and VADs now swelled the ranks of professional nurses, but through 1914-15 voluntary bodies directing other branches of war work for women proliferated. On 17 July 1915, Mrs Pankhurst and David Lloyd George, the future Prime Minister, headed the Women's Right to Serve March through London, advertising the urgent necessity for women to take over men's jobs. Lucy's sister Edith was among those commissioned to produce posters encouraging women to work in munitions. Munition work was well paid and, though not without hazards, appealed to a wide cross-section of the population. By 1916 women were employed in the police and extensively on the land, while early in 1917 the military introduced women's auxiliary corps, an

Sketch for ***Forward the Guns.*** *Oil, 6½in x 11in. Probably one of the preliminary oil sketches which Lucy described in her diary for September 1916.*

innovation Lucy cheered, "The most exciting news I've heard for a long time".

For horses, too, the war brought change. By 1911 the London General Omnibus Company was phasing out its horse-drawn vehicles and others would soon follow suit. The army had been experimenting with motors since the Boer War, but the entrenchment of the Western Front rapidly made cavalry superfluous and primitive tanks appeared. Although in the war of movement in the Middle East Allenby's victory was largely due to the quality and fitness of his cavalry, the occasional specific manoeuvres for which they were used in France, such as in the Battle of Cambrai in 1917, were largely unsuccessful. The army was on the brink of mechanisation, with troops sometimes being transported up the line in fleets of motorised buses, and motorised ambulances,

Forward the Guns. *Oil on canvas, 60in x 120in. Exhibited at the Royal Academy, 1917. Lucy attempted repeatedly and unsuccessfully to get to France as an ambulance driver, a nurse or a war artist. Her best-known war picture was therefore painted in frustration near Bulford Camp on Salisbury Plain during the autumn of 1916.*

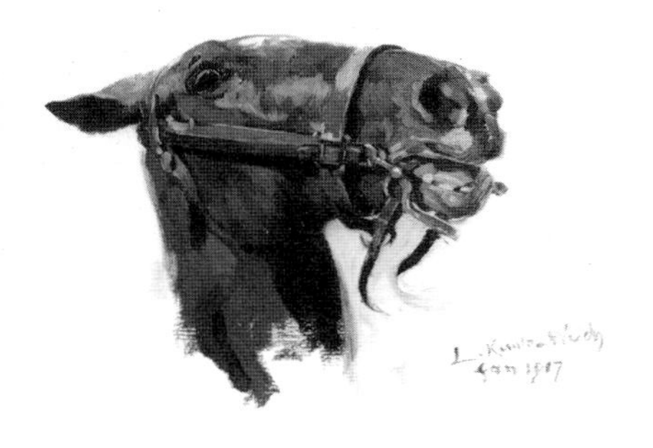

Study for ***Forward the Guns.*** *Oil on board, 10in x 14in. Back in Bushey Lucy borrowed a horse from a neighbour, Mr. Price, and on 4 January 1917 completed an oil study for the rearing lead horse which she incorporated into the Academy version the following day. This study was bought from Lucy after the War by Philip Dennison.*

driven by women, increasingly in evidence as the War progressed.

Nevertheless, horses were still essential for hauling guns, carting supplies and maintaining communications in the worst conditions. The consumption of ammunition alone was phenomenal, 2,000,000 shells being expended by the French and British in seven days of the Battle of the Somme in 1916[24] and the logistics of supplying such a vast army over so long a front intensified the demand for horses. Donkeys were sometimes used to distribute rations or small ammunition along trench systems, while the Army Service Corps employed mules. In April 1916 Lucy watched a convoy of 130 mule wagons passing through Seaford for Newhaven Docks. Needless to say she followed in search of a possible subject. Armaments apart, shipments of food, clothing, blankets, catering equipment and medical supplies to France were enormous. Baden-Powell was stunned that the British goods-shed at Le Havre covered sixteen acres,[25] and all its contents had to be transported by rail or horse. The Army increased its establishment from 25,000 horses in 1914 to 869,931 in 1917. The Boer War may not have prepared troops for this appalling static warfare, but it had taught them to look after their animals properly. By October 1917 British horse losses on the Western Front amounted to 256,204, less than half the French total and, though once again most died through disease and poor conditions rather than enemy action, nevertheless the animals were often better treated than the men.[26]

In November 1914, before it was appreciated how ineffective the cavalry would prove, the Parliamentary Recruiting Committee contacted Lucy with an idea for a poster of a cavalryman charging straight at the viewer. It had been proposed originally by Captain de Villas Boas and Lucy submitted her drawings in August 1915. She was not particularly satisfied with them but she had had a busy year, with *Black Beauty* occupying much of her time. In addition, an accident to her knee had put her on crutches, drastically curtailing her activities and preventing

24. John Laffin, *The Western Front Illustrated 1914-18*, 1991.
25. Tim Jeal, *Baden-Powell*, 1989, p.453.
26. The War Office, *Statistics of the Military Effort of the British Empire during the Great War 1914-1920*, 1922, p.396-7. Also, E.H. Edwards, *Horses, Their Role in the History of Mankind*, 1987.

Women's Work in the Great War 1914–1918*. Canvas panel, 216in x 132in, 1924. Lucy's tribute to her contemporaries whom she depicted in various roles and uniforms, picking up the tools abandoned by the men marching off to war.*

Troops and Horses in the Midday Shade. *Oil on canvas, 31½in x 40¾in, c.1916. Lucy, like most other civilians, was fascinated by troop movements and activities.*

her from riding for months. The poster was finally completed after Rowland Wheelwright, formerly assistant master in Lucy's school, posed for the horseman and the Committee had sent photographs of the correct equipment. Rather inappropriately, since he was gun-shy, Black Prince modelled for the charger. The poster was immediately popular and all remaining stock was sold off after the War.

Conscription in 1916 put an end to the recruiting campaign. With its calls upon civilians, the War invaded daily life as the fighting in South Africa, thousands of miles away, never had. Lucy noted the blast at 7.00 p.m. which wrecked the Venesta munitions factory at Silvertown on 19 January 1917, and that autumn from Bushey High Street villagers watched the air raids on London. There were days when they could even hear the guns in Flanders. Spy fever ran high too, and in June 1915 Lucy was summoned to the police station where two students were under arrest, having been caught sketching Watford Bridge. Although Lucy reprimanded these pupils sharply for their stupidity, she speculated on troop movements herself and was not above searching out their encampments. A close friend, Harold Paris, was in the Royal Artillery and whenever she heard his

battery would be moving locally she set off on BP to observe them en route. In fact Paris' experiences with the gun teams, which Lucy had followed since December 1915, were probably the inspiration behind her next undertaking, 'Forward the Guns' (RA 1917).

News of the horrendous casualties at the Battle of the Somme on 1 July, however, halted her preparations. From 4 July she hammered on doors in Whitehall, offering her services at the Front but met with endless rejections. When she appealed to *The Graphic* to be sent out under their auspices, with or without a permit to draw, she had no better luck, although within months the Canadian Government appointed her male colleagues, Munnings and Algernon Talmage, Official War Artists. She enrolled for a first aid course, then tried the French Red Cross for whom Jane and Wilfrid de Glehn, John Masefield and Henry Tonks were working in the Marne. The French also refused. To add to her frustration, other women seemingly encountered no such difficulties. A Bushey neighbour, Elsie Higgins, had been repatriated recently from France after an accident, while only days before Lucy Lockwood, a former pupil, had been accepted to drive ambulances. Similarly, Olave Baden-Powell apparently travelled back and forth with ease for the Scout

The Hon. Elydir Herbert, VC. *Charcoal 24¾in x 18¾in. Lucy's charcoal study for the memorial picture of Lord Treowen's son in the action at Huj in the Middle East where he died on 8 November 1917.*

Gun Carriage Horses. *Oil on canvas, 10in x 8in, 1916. On 11 September, 1916, Colonel Yorke arranged for Captain Bonamy Dobree to pose with two horses in the yard at Bulford Camp.*

Soldiers Resting. *Watercolour, 11in x 9¾in. Access to troops in training, albeit not in France, allowed Lucy to capture some spontaneously humorous moments.*

Association. In September Lucy appealed to her for advice, but all to no avail.

She resumed her studies of the artillery practising at Woolwich, but little work was being done with horse teams there. Towards the end of August, therefore, she set off for Salisbury Plain where she found Larkhill and Bulford Camps full of Australians. Colonel Yorke readily gave Lucy permission to paint the batteries as they exercised and went out of his way to help, sending a car to take her out to the ranges where she could observe the field gun teams manoeuvring at speed. On other occasions he arranged for horses and men to model for her in the yard. She had to work fast to take advantage of this unusual access and on her first morning in the field she managed to make "a lightning quick sketch of the whole thing in oil and came home at 12.30". After ten days, she had her big picture case erected on the Plain and she worked there determinedly until term started in October. By way of thanks she left the Colonel a painting of his horse and a pencil sketch for Captain Bonamy Dobree as well. When her picture arrived back at Bushey she discovered that the courteous Colonel had even paid its carriage for her.

Lucy battled to finish the picture in time for the Royal Academy in 1917. As late as February in her studio she was removing large areas of pigment with chloroform

Forward to Victory – Enlist Now. *Poster, 1915. Based on designs submitted to the Parliamentary Recruiting Committee by a serving officer, Lucy used Rowland Wheelwright, assistant master at her school, and Black Prince as her models.*

Sketch for ***The Straw Ride*** *(pages 14-15). Oil on panel, 12½in x 29in, 1919-20. The Women's Work Sub-Committee had rejected this composition when Lucy showed it to them originally but changed their mind after the finished work was well received at the RA in 1920.*

to repaint them and only added the harness to the leading horse after the picture had been shown publicly in Bushey. She felt that in her rush the picture was only half done. Unhappy with the result, she consoled herself as she packed it up that at least, while the conflicting directional forces threatened to pull the composition apart, the frame might help to pull it together. However, her anxiety was unnecessary. The next day a confidential letter from Joe Farquharson, who had pipped her in the Royal Academy elections, assured her that it had been greatly admired and by the end of the month it had been purchased by the Chantrey Bequest. It was rare indeed for an artist to be singled out twice in this way.

To some extent this was due to timing. Lucy had delivered a very upbeat message. She depicted the troop as she had seen it exercising at Bulford, without any helmets and going into action at speed over dry ground. At this stage, unbelievably, the British artillery was still training for warfare on eighteenth century lines and was less accurate and competent than either the French or the Germans. Once the ground in Flanders was churned up and waterlogged it took not the minimum of six, but as many as ten or twelve horses to drag the artillery pieces into position and sometimes the guns had to be dug out of the mire by hand. Nevertheless, only access to the Front, as artist, ambulance driver or nurse, could have given Lucy the insight to penetrate 'the old lie' of Wilfrid Owen's poetry. Instead, as in Lucy's most successful pictures, the teams in 'Forward the Guns' are breasting a hill. Charging forward out of the smoke and dust and urged on by the officer on the right, the horses' momentum is only impeded momentarily by the leading horse rearing up, panicked by an exploding shell. The image was so powerful and emotive that the British public could almost hear the thundering hooves, the jangling harness, the trundling guns, the deafening barrage, the sound of victory.

Colonel Yorke reported that his brigade was delighted with the result, soldiers pausing in front of the canvas at Burlington House were overheard admiring it and a reproduction was quickly put in hand. Lucy's celebrations, however, were short-lived. The criticism when it came was not from the military and had

In Hoc Signo Spes Mea. *Crayon with white highlights, 16in x 10¾in, 1918. This was the motto of Durban Taff.*

Lucem Spero. *Charcoal with highlights, 16¼in x 10¾in.* Lucem Spero *(I hope for light) was the Kemp familiy motto, which Lucy put to topical use in 1918. Her grandfather, Martin Kemp, had added his mother's maiden name, Welch, to his own to perpetuate that branch of the family.*

nothing to do with authenticity. It was from the art lobby and Lucy was the innocent victim of their justifiable anger. A row had been brewing over the Royal Academy's administration of the Chantrey Bequest Fund since 1904, when a House of Lords' Select Committee had recommended changes. Although Sir Francis Chantrey's will had requested that sculpture and works of art executed in Britain should be purchased for the nation, the Academicians had restricted their purchases almost exclusively to Academy exhibits, thereby ignoring works shown elsewhere, such as the New English Art Club or the International Society. The purchase of a second work by a painter already represented in the national collection was the spark which lit the tinder. Writing in the *The Observer* on 22 July 1917, the art critic P.G. Konody commented that the Tate Gallery Trustees were thinking of refusing the picture in order to make it clear that "they were not a dumping ground for the Board's injudicious purchases".

Championed by members of the Academy, particularly David Murray, Lucy started libel proceedings, but *The Observer* was slow to print a somewhat guarded apology. Whether or not Konody's attack was intended personally, there

Early Morning Ride at Russley. *Oil on canvas, 9½in x 12½in, 1919. Lucy followed the grooms' daily routine at Russley as part of her preliminary research for the commission from the Women's Work Sub-Committee.*

would probably have been queries over any Chantrey purchase that year, as it was the first time the Tate Gallery had been given the chance to vet the selection, but Lucy refused to meet Konody when he called at Kingsley to explain himself. The legal wrangle added a twist to the stream of rejections she had now received from Whitehall where she had applied again recently and unsuccessfully through John Buchan at the Foreign Office to go to France.

Although her painting was eventually accepted by the Tate Gallery Trustees, Lucy was immensely distressed by the hostility which the affair had disclosed. It was disconcerting to be dispensed with so ignominiously by both the establishment and the art world. Work was once again the panacea and throughout the summer, without the heart to look further afield for fresh subjects, she persevered with her studies of the artillery. She had in mind, to contrast with the fast-paced 'Forward the Guns', a study of a heavy gun being pulled by shires. These great guns, cumbersome even in dry conditions, sometimes required fourteen or sixteen heavy horses to pull them through mud, and while making the preparatory sketches of the Royal Artillery training at Morn Hill Camp, Magdon Hill and the

Preparatory sketch for ***Exercise.*** *Oil on canvas, 16¼in x 24in. Cecil Aldin, artist and remount officer, claimed that women could train remounts more efficiently, quickly and gently, than most male grooms he had employed.*

Exercise. *Oil on canvas, 44in x 58½in, 1919. Lucy was officially commissioned by the Women's Work Sub-Committee of the Imperial War Museum to visit Russley Park in Wiltshire before all the remount depots were closed and to record the women's exceptional achievements in training army remounts.*

Punchbowl near Winchester, Lucy decided to set her picture in the snow. The popularity of 'Forward the Guns' nationally ensured she was given every assistance by the regiment and their commanding officer, Colonel Parker. Yet even this turned sour. After 'Big Guns Up To The Front' was shown at the Academy in 1918, the officers asked to have it reproduced in colour. Lucy arranged this, but as the print was not ready for subscription until after demobilisation she was left with them all on her hands. They were eventually sold with the picture to the National Museum of Wales in 1921.

The sale was brokered for Lucy by Lord Treown, a Museum Trustee who lived at Llanarth Court in Raglan. It was out of affection for him and his wife that Lucy later undertook her least characteristic commission, a memorial picture of their son, Captain the Hon Elydir Herbert. He had been posthumously awarded the VC for his bravery in capturing a machine gun and turning it against the enemy to protect the 5th Mounted Brigade at Huj in the Middle East on 8 November 1917.[27] The painting's presentation in September 1923 was a lavish affair with over five hundred guests and speeches which, as Lucy said, "harrowed everyone thoroughly".

More cheering, if a little galling since her own efforts had been so frustrated, was the commission to commemorate 'Women's Work in the Great War' for the Empress Club in Dover Street, of which she was a member. In fact, the Emergency Voluntary Aid Committee formed there in August 1914 had been one of the bodies through which she had applied to serve at the Front in 1916. Although their idea of funding the final panel in the Royal Exchange was first mooted in November 1917 Lucy did not embark on the designs until the autumn of 1919, after which the painting was somewhat vexed by her ill-health. The picture was eighteen feet high, and a middle ear infection, affecting her balance, prevented her climbing the scaffolding. The process was further complicated by the Empress Club wanting a large copy made for themselves at the same time. By sheer chance, in 1921, a former pupil, Marguerite Frobisher, applied to Lucy for a job and after acting as a secretary she gradually took over the administration of the school. She also modelled for several of the figures in the panel, which depicted ten women against a backdrop of the sea picking up the tools abandoned by the men marching off to war. The painting was finally installed at the Royal Exchange and unveiled by Princess Mary on 28 April 1924.

The panel encompassed women's work in the army, navy, land army, and as nurses, teachers, munitioneers and mothers but it was through another 'women's work' project that she encountered the female remount hands with whose war work she would identify most closely. In 1919 she was asked by Lady Norman of the official Women's Work Sub-Committee at the Imperial War Museum to record the activities of the Ladies' Army Remount Depot at Russley Park in Wiltshire before it was disbanded. After all Lucy's vain attempts to get to France as a war artist, Lady Norman and Agnes Conway were now actively engaging female artists to record women's contributions before it was too late. Anna Airy, for instance, was

27. The Marquess of Anglesey, *A History of the British Cavalry*, Vol.5, 1994.

Women grooms at Russley.

given several commissions covering munitions and aircraft factories in March 1919, while Olive Edis was the only woman photographer authorised to tour the battlefields immediately after the war.[28] Visiting Russley on 13 March 1919 Lucy saw so many potential subjects that she accepted the commission at a reduced rate, provided she was allowed to paint something for herself as well.

Since Lucy had painted remounts during the Boer War, it seems curious that she took so long to discover them this time, particularly as they now depended largely on female grooms. The artist and huntsman, Cecil Aldin, who ran the remount depot at Calcot Park near Reading during the War, claimed to have been the first Remount Officer to replace stable-boys with women. In 1917 Munnings had joined Aldin at Calcot Park for a period before he went overseas, but Aldin had no shortage of women and girls applying to work with the horses. He was impressed at how much more quickly and speedily than men the women controlled and prepared frequently cantankerous arrivals for issue, so that gradually more and more depots throughout the country were placed under female supervision. It was, as Lucy had described in 'Young April' and 'The Riders', down to women's conciliatory, horse-centred, approach. Russley, where female grooms had been translating horses into heroes daily since 1915, embodied the philosophy she lived and painted.

In spite of this, the whole commission was bedevilled with frustrations, not least of which was that she had come upon Russley just as it was closing down. Making up for lost time, she joined the camp's activities in March and the working title she gave her own picture, 'Amazons', revealed her respect both for the women and the horses. The transformation she had effected with BP, these girls were now achieving with hundreds of difficult horses a month. Unhappily however, her sojourn at Russley was of short duration. During May Edith had an operation for breast cancer and Lucy could not return to Wiltshire until June.

By early 1920 she had completed several Russley paintings, including the Imperial War Museum's modest study of the horses at 'Exercise' and her own large

28. Diana Condell and Jean Liddiard, *Working for Victory?*, 1987.

The Waitress. *Pastel, 8¼in x 11¼in. Although she was not included in the finished painting, this 'nippy' at Lyons Corner House was one of many women whom Lucy recorded for* ***Women's Work in the Great War*** *(page 121).*

Academy exhibit, now re-titled 'The Straw Ride' (RA 1920) and priced at £1,000. A huge *contre-jour* composition of horses being galloped in pairs round the indoor school, the size, rhythm, and structural strength of the composition put the Sub-Committee's commission in the shade. While Agnes Conway told Lucy that 'The Straw Ride' would dwarf the other pictures in their collection, Lady Norman accused Lucy of devoting more effort to her picture than to theirs and asked to have it instead. Lucy was particularly annoyed, because Lady Norman had rejected a smaller, preliminary version of 'The Straw Ride'. Furthermore, it appeared that she now expected to buy the larger picture for the cut price of the smaller one, £150. Eventually Lucy compromised, making an outright gift of 'The Straw Ride' to the Museum in addition to selling the Women's Work Sub-Committee 'Exercise' as agreed. Nevertheless, it was another unsettling incident.

The War had converted not just horses, but women, into heroes and in December 1918 women over thirty with the appropriate property qualifications voted for the first time in a British General Election. For Lucy exceptionally, however, having fought so hard to contribute, the War had ended not in emancipation, but in disappointment and restrictions. Her confidence had taken a severe knocking and, like the well-schooled remount ponies, she was now facing a much-changed world.

CHAPTER NINE

"A Friend in Need"

New Year's Night *(Black Beauty, 1915)*

'Horses as Friends'

The earliest and most obvious changes were closest to home. In October 1919, when Lucy reopened the school, which had been closed during the later part of the War, there were only four girls on the register. Not only had the War presented women with many alternatives, but Lucy was not a born teacher and the school had suffered several metamorphoses under her management. She had taken the enterprise over from Herkomer almost as a package, comprising everything from the buildings to the rules, and when she re-launched it in January 1905 as 'The Bushey School of Painting' Rowland Wheelwright and John Whiteley were the assistant masters and Harry Goffey the secretary.

From the outset, it had been an almost constant headache. Within months there were problems, with students stealing and poison pen letters. Begrudging the teaching time, Lucy's attendance was irregular and pupils had found it easy to play hookey. Her diary recorded how she rode out on Black Prince searching, often in vain, for students who were meant to be painting in the neighbourhood. They amused themselves by hiding at her approach. On one sketching trip to Litlington in Sussex, for instance, this game of cat and mouse

---

The death of Black Prince, Lucy's model for Black Beauty, at Baden-Powell's home in October 1923, was one of several events which marked difficult and changing times ahead for Lucy after the War.

went on for several days. It had been a relief, therefore, in July 1911 to sell the buildings back to Herkomer who demolished them the following year and planted a rose garden on the site. The only remaining member of staff, Rowland Wheelwright, left. Lucy moved the reduced school and the glass studio to Rudolph Road and re-named it 'The Kemp-Welch School'. By 1919, with classes smaller still, lessons seem to have been organised mainly in the glasshouse studio and when Marguerite Frobisher became Lucy's secretary in 1920 she took over most of the day to day running of the school. In 1922 the name was changed finally to 'The Kemp-Welch School for Drawing and Painting'.[30]

Meanwhile, the question of Lucy's election to the Academy came up again. In recent years other women had also been nominated, Annie Swynnerton, an older, Pre-Raphaelite, painter in 1914, Laura Knight in 1915 and Anna Airy in 1919. A change to the Academy's constitution in 1919 meant that, whereas previously a candidate once proposed for election had remained on the books permanently, a time limit of seven years was now imposed. Lucy's earlier nomination, dating from 1900, was renewed therefore in 1920, as was Annie Swynnerton's, but for Lucy disappointment was in store. When in 1922, after nearly one hundred and twenty years, the Academy finally risked electing a female ARA, they chose Annie Swynnerton. Gradually, imperceptibly, Lucy was sidelined. In 1927, when Laura Knight was elected,

30. Grant Longman, *Schools of Art in South West Hertfordshire*, Hertfordshire Local History Council, 1991.

Lucy's nomination was renewed for the last time. In 1934, when Dod Procter was admitted, Lucy's nomination lapsed completely.

Laura Knight and Dod Procter were both married to painters and undoubtedly many women artists were greatly advantaged by the advocacy of their artist menfolk, be they husbands, fathers or brothers. Although Lucy had many friends and admirers among the Royal Academicians, who now included several Bushey contemporaries such as George Harcourt, Arnesby Brown and Algernon Talmage, she did not play politics or solicit favours. Indeed, sometimes she was her own worst enemy, making a poor showing at the Royal Academy in 1919, for example, when she was busy at Russley and Edith was ill. One of her exhibits then was a privately commissioned horse-racing picture, 'Silks and Satins, Goodwood'. It was an unsympathetic choice of subject for her and

Following the Plough. *Oil on canvas, 20in x 25in. Successfully re-working the earlier image of* ***Ploughing on the South Coast,*** *this canvas probably dates from Lucy's visit to Cornwall after the First World War.*

earned a rebuke from David Murray, previously one of her foremost supporters. Once regarded as the epitome of emancipated womanhood, her early success had been of her own making, yet she had not courted the role unduly and was out of step with the post-war art world. It seems particularly ironic that, having promoted the cause of women so constructively through her hard-working independence, she should benefit so little from its achievement in the end. Nevertheless, as other younger women asserted themselves, Lucy continued as before to take her characteristic line, putting horses and painting first.

To her private work rather than public commissions, however, the aftermath of war brought positive changes of tempo and outlook. In August 1919, when she was devoting most of her energies to the memorial paintings, she took Edith to Cornwall to recuperate after her mastectomy operation. It was a respite for Lucy too, the first time for several years that she had been able to devote her attention unreservedly to farming pictures, and the Cornish light inspired a clutch of jewelled canvases. It was as if she had emerged from the tunnel of war into a brightly coloured world where her pigments glowed against the

The Glory of the Setting Sun. *Oil on canvas, 28in x 26in. Painted at Cadgwith where Lucy had taken Edith to convalesce during 1919. The visit to Cornwall enabled Lucy to resume her exploration of light, colour and reflections in the aftermath of war and revealed her new found admiration for Monet.*

backdrop of a brilliant sea. Even the titles responded in colour, 'August Blue' and 'The Sapphire Sea'. Painted on and around the cliffs above the Lizard, their concentrated vitality recalled the images she had discovered in Sussex before the War. Although this was only an interlude, by October she had virtually completed eight pictures, refreshing antidotes to the formal, institutional chores waiting in her studio.

Among the largest of the eight, 'The Glory of the Setting Sun', set in the harbour at Cadgwith, updated the concept of 'The Incoming Tide' using a stronger palette and flickering brush-strokes. A comparison between the two suggests that Lucy's original interest in the gulls, triggered by their noisy, acrobatic flight, had been replaced by a fascination with the vibrant reflections of sunlight on the water. How much of this was due to colour becoming physically more important as her sight altered with age and how much to a greater awareness of Impressionist and Post-Impressionist paintings would be difficult to judge. Lucy's idea that light gave unity and purpose to objects was the reverse of the Impressionist idea that objects describe the quality of light.

The Afternoon Ride. *Oil on board. 13in x 16¼in. Bill (Vyvyan) Musgrave Clark on 'Belka'. Lucy met Bill's future wife, Audrey Thorne, at Russley in 1919 and thereafter visited their Arab studfarm in Sussex frequently.*

However, she had been delighted when Lord Vernon's collection of 19th century French paintings, particularly the works by Monet, were shown at the National Gallery in 1917.

For Black Prince, too, life was changing. Back in Bushey later in 1919 a film crew appeared, eager to capture the artist at work. It was mid-November, but Lucy and BP were hauled out into a field where she "shrivelled" with cold all day, pretending to paint on one of the stag-hunting canvases. This was Black Prince's last starring role. In June 1922 Baden-Powell brought his daughter to Bushey to meet his erstwhile charger with whom, through Dent's *Black Beauty*, she had already made friends. Soon after, it was agreed that Black Prince should return to their home, Pax Hill at Bentley in Hampshire, for his holidays when Lucy was away. By the end of the following summer, 1923, it was clear Black Prince was failing. Baden-Powell sent Lucy regular bulletins leading up to the old horse's death on 28 October. Podger, too, had died in 1910, another fragment of the past disintegrating, but new horses and new friends were now

Carthorses on the Track. *Watercolour 5¼in x 9½in. One of Lucy's illustrations for Raphael Tuck's* Farm Pictures *in 1936. Although it echoes* ***The Laggard*** *in part, this watercolour with its free-flying birds conveys a increased awareness of wind and weather.*

entering Lucy's life.

In March 1920, Audrey Thorne, one of the Russley girls, contacted Lucy wanting to buy the oil sketch Lucy had made of her wearing a red headscarf. It was to be a present for her fiancé, 'Bill', Vyvyan Musgrave Clark, a breeder of Arab horses. The letter initiated a friendship lasting many years. After Thorne's marriage in 1920 Lucy visited their stud in Sussex where they tried, unrewardingly on occasions, to find work for some of the ex-Russley grooms. Bill had bought his first Arab stallion from the Blunts at Crabbet Park in 1910 and was a founder member of the Arab Horse Society in 1918. In 1925 he asked Lucy to paint Audrey on Belka, a grey mare which became famous for her long distance wins in 1920-21. The finished commission, 'On The South Downs', was exhibited at the Royal Academy the following year. Lucy also painted Bill riding Belka and subsequently depicted some of their other horses, Arabs and hunters, among them Feluca, Curlew, Katerfelto and Dynamite. In October 1925, two years after Black Prince's death, they sent Lucy Mustapha Kamel, a bay stallion foaled in 1906 and bred by Lady Anne Blunt by Feysul ex Mabsuta.[31] His Arab docility was quite a departure after Black Prince's antics, and he stood patiently to be painted, Lucy holding his long rein lightly in the same hand as her palette.

Small, elegant and characteristically dish-faced, the Arab is a legendary breed with a wealth of exotic history. Through her association with the Musgrave

31. Peter Upton, 1985.

A Cornish Harvesting. *Oil, 16in x 20in. Completed* en plein air *at the Lizard between August and October 1919, this was among the series of canvases which Lucy contributed to the Animal Painters' Exhibition at the Fine Art Society in November that year. The intensity of its pigments reflects how dramatically Lucy responded to the colour of Cornwall that summer.*

Clarks and the Arab Horse Society, Lucy went on to paint a number of Arab horses and their owners, among them Elizabeth Usborne and her Arab in 1926 and Rosemary Bromley on Rythama in 1935. Miss Bromley was the niece of Lucy's distant cousins, Mr and Mrs Mountain, who lived at Groombridge Place in Kent. They were very good to Edith during the inter-war years when her health was failing and she was frequently their guest when Lucy was travelling. Lucy meanwhile was also introduced to Lady Yule whose Hanstead Stud was close to Bushey, at St Albans. In 1931 Lucy painted 'A Lady of Quality' there, featuring the Arab mare and foal, Razina and Razzia. A portrait of Gladys Yule on Sirocco followed in 1933 and a study of Le Phare in 1934. Although many friends prevailed upon Lucy for portrait commissions during this period, she was never quite comfortable with the artifice involved. Other breeders commented that she failed to appreciate, or rather did not convey, the special characteristics of the Arab, although she kept Mustapha for at least ten years. With his white blaze he made a handsome escort but, though he had been shown successfully for several years before he came to Lucy, he was not necessarily a typical Arab. Moreover, horse breeding was not, and had never

Above the Cove. *Oil on board, 6¾in x 11in. Lucy's habitual preoccupation with horses was balanced by her growing interest in light.*

been, a priority for Lucy. Her particular skill as a horse painter had been based not on tracing bloodlines for posterity, and therefore highlighting specific traits, such as small head, curved neck, high tail, slim legs, but in treating every horse as an individual. To Lucy, Mustapha was primarily a friend, not an example of the Arab breed with points to be enumerated.

The End of the Day. *Canvas laid down, 8¼in x 11½in. Another in the series of jewelled canvases which emerged from Lucy's visit to the Cornish coast in August 1919.*

Patience. *Canvas 8in x 9¼in. The deep shadows and Lucy's low viewpoint throw this heavy horse into monumental relief against its sketchy background.*

This was equally her attitude to thoroughbred horses. She was more interested in how horses differed from the norm than in how they conformed and it was this which gave her paintings their particular appeal:

> "I am often asked 'Why do you not paint the horse in its perfection, the thoroughbred horse?' I am not quite sure that I know why myself; is it not that perfection in its cultivated form is not paintable and from the artist's point of view uninteresting... The thoroughbred horse is known to move in a certain manner, its form, appearance, actions and everything are understood and tabulated. Now what is left in this case for the painter who, poor thing would like a little something left to him to do but who must not deviate from this perfectly understood form by a single hair? Now this type is always interesting – I mean the natural type, fashioned by nature and not by man – full of faults, variable, beautiful, and lovable beyond words."

Lucy painting Mustapha.

She still felt more at ease as a painter with the down to earth working subjects which had established her reputation. Significantly, for a large oil of the Hanstead hayfields which Lady Yule commissioned in 1933, Lucy charged £400, twice as much as her fee for the painting of Gladys on Sirocco and more than four times as much as her usual charges for portraits. The fee reflected not only Lucy's confidence in her paintings of this type but the continuing, even growing, demand for them. By the thirties, her various farming scenes had acquired added piquancy as records of a way of life under threat. It was not just mechanisation. Although that was already having considerable effect in towns, the Depression ensured that in spite of technological advances, few farmers could afford to replace horses with machines just yet. Even in 1939, horses were still supplying two-thirds of agricultural power. In fact, the greatest menace to rural life was the spread of metroland which was rapidly devouring former villages, such as Bushey, on the outskirts of London.

It was against this background that Lucy returned to timber-hauling subjects, hunting them down during the early twenties in Wales, then in Ashdown Forest in Sussex and in 1934 closer to home at Markyate. These paintings bore further witness to the change of pace in Lucy's most personal work. The canvases, now

In The Sunset. *Oil on canvas, 9½in x 8in. Billie and June, the retired work horses who came to live at Kingsley, featured in many of Lucy's post-war studies of white horses against different lights and backgrounds.*

Breeze Across the Cornlands. *Oil on canvas, 28in x 36in. Alternatively entitled* ***The Longest Way****, this picture was purchased by Philip Dennison in 1939. The central idea of heavy horses being magnified against a reduced background was more emblematic than realistic and Lucy seems to have employed it first in* ***Ho, for the Western Wind*** *around 1931.*

more modest in size, rejoiced in sure, liberated brushwork and luminous light and colour. This was evident too in some of her farming pictures, notably 'Breeze Across the Cornlands'. A fresh handling of the downland farming images, this picture depicted the horse-team not just cresting the summit but magnified half-length with the landscape reduced behind them as if they transcended their labour. Although the tackle restrains them, reining them into their work, nevertheless the wind ruffling their manes implies the wildness of their nature and their indomitable spirit. It has all the vibrance of 'Colt Hunting' encased in the stability of the Cocking pictures.

Lucy explored this windswept motif repeatedly at this time in various situations using alternatively farm horses, Arabs or moorland ponies, with titles such as 'Breeze at the Gate', 'Breeze and Broad Spaces' or 'Ho for the Western Wind'. Descending in a direct line from 'Colt Hunting' through 'The Joy of Life' to the headpieces for *Black Beauty*, these horse heads in the wind dispensed with any tenuous narrative and became Lucy's final expression of the freedom-restraint theme, the bias towards freedom becoming increasingly evident with time.

'Breeze Across the Cornlands' was bought by Philip Dennison, a young

Horses working by an East Coast Estuary. *Canvas laid down, 9½in x 13in, c.1937. Possibly an oil study for a larger painting set above the backwaters of the Naze.*

Canadian officer who turned up at Bushey in 1919 to have a print signed. Between the Wars he built up a small collection of Lucy's work, oils as well as drawings, and wrote occasionally with specific instructions for a commission. 'The Guardian' for instance, a study of a horse with two children, was Lucy's response

Over the Fence. *Charcoal, 13¾in x 16in. Lucy's growing interest in colour and light during the twenties gave rise to the many white horses and snow scenes which she explored in various media, even charcoal.*

O Shepherd of the Hills. *Oil on canvas, 28in x 36in. Exhibited at the Royal Academy, 1929. Although mechanisation began slowly to erode the horse's ascendancy on farms before the Second World War, there were still some jobs, particularly in snowy conditions, which horses handled better than contemporary tractors.*

to his request for a painting based on one of the horses she had painted in 'The Road to Exeter'. Elsewhere in the Colonies, in South Africa and Australia, Lucy's paintings had already found their way into museums. In New Zealand Edwin Murray Fuller was instrumental in selling a number of her pictures between 1928 and 1933 through his touring exhibitions of contemporary British Art. In 1929, some of Lucy's paintings were lost at sea when the S.S. *Manuka* foundered near Dunedin with a consignment for Murray Fuller on board.[32]

Lucy's pictures were valued in the Colonies as reminders of 'home' but for Lucy, at home, finding models was no longer easy. She herself had taken driving lessons in the hope of going to France as an ambulance driver in January 1916. In any event by the twenties it was no longer simply a matter of walking up Bushey High Street and borrowing a horse from a neighbour for a few days, although Express Dairies still kept six horses nearby. In 1924 therefore Lucy bought an old grey van horse, Billie, from Pearkes the drapers in Watford. Billie was followed later by June, a white cart-horse put out to grass by a brewery. June was a stalwart friend to Lucy and together they grew stout with age. June would carry artist,

32. Neil Roberts, Robert McDougall Art Gallery, Christchurch.

The Team. *Watercolour, 8in x 8½in. Lucy's watercolours of working horses became increasingly atmospheric through the twenties and thirties.*

canvas, easel, paintbox and other impedimenta willingly to all sorts of painting places but she heartily disliked Mustapha and would not share his stable.

June and Billie probably served as models for some of the snow-bound farming scenes with which Lucy started to experiment, having finished the memorial commissions. She had realised snow's painterly qualities when

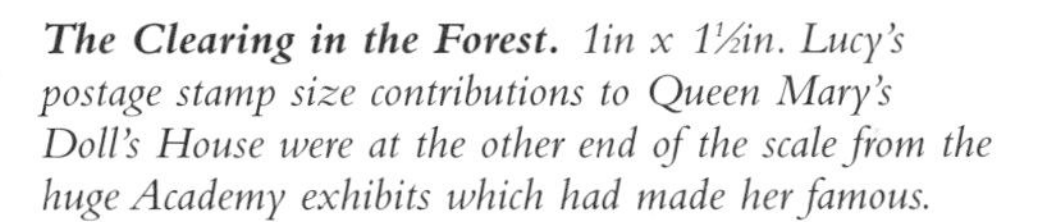

The Clearing in the Forest. *1in x 1½in. Lucy's postage stamp size contributions to Queen Mary's Doll's House were at the other end of the scale from the huge Academy exhibits which had made her famous.*

Harvest of the Woods. *Oil on canvas, 16in x 23in. Lucy returned to timber-hauling subjects as the spread of Metroland between the wars threatened the British countryside.*

On a Sunset Cliff. *Canvas 6½in x 10½in. Painted in Cornwall, 1919.*

Lighting Up Time. *Pastel, 12in x 16in, c.1927-31. This pastel, probably executed in Sussex, is primarily a study in colour and atmosphere.*

planning 'Big Guns Up to the Front' in 1918 and perhaps was drawn back to it again when Princess Marie Louise asked her to contribute to Queen Mary's Dolls' House, designed by Sir Edwin Lutyens for the British Empire Exhibition in 1924. She reproduced a tiny version of the 'Big Guns' picture then, as well as a miniature timber-hauling watercolour. Lucy's snow pictures, extending from 1924 into the early thirties, slightly pre-dated the period when Munnings too was painting in the snow. They offer a further illustration of the post-war shift in Lucy's outlook. Part of their attraction for Lucy appears to have been the shadows and reflections which the snow created. On one occasion after it had melted, she draped white sheets under a horse's ribs to imitate the tones of the lost light. Setting her students to paint a white horse against the sky from a low view point she reminded them: "The first things to be noticed in painting a white horse are the small amount of actual white and the warm, green colour of the shadows."

The sequence also exposed the harshness of rural life in which men, horses and, in Lucy's case, artists were pitted against the climate. In snowy conditions horses could still prevail over machines but mechanisation was now eroding their territory so fast that Lucy could scarcely keep up with it. In fact, progress completely overtook a subject suggested to her by Edward Seago – the team of horses which he had watched launching a lifeboat at Brook, on the Isle of

The Well-Beloved. *Watercolour, 15in x 14in. A study of Carole Birkbeck, with her hair tied back in a headscarf like the grooms at Russley. This watercolour was not exhibited at the RI until 1939.*

Turning at the Cliff Edge. *Canvas, 7½in x 10½in. This small sketch illustrates how Lucy used not just the colour but the texture of the oil paint to bring life and movement to her work.*

Wight. By September 1937, when he had persuaded Lucy that she was better qualified to paint this than he, the Brook lifeboat had been motorised and the last horse-drawn lifeboat in Britain, at Wells in Norfolk, had been out of service for nearly a year. Nevertheless, with the encouragement of Seago and Lord Mottistone, the Isle of Wight Lifeboat chairman, Lucy eventually painted 'A Call from the Sea', amalgamating elements from the Brook, Worthing and Newhaven boats. As a topic painting and a huge canvas some eight feet in length, it was a rare undertaking for Lucy by this time, but Seago had insisted that only Lucy, painting on the large scale, could do the subject justice before it disappeared forever. It was an amazing *tour de force*, the strength and vigour of the canvas belying her age. Nevertheless, although it was selected it was not hung at the Royal Academy in 1939 and was the last of her major works.

She had encountered Seago in her capacity as President of the Society of Animal Painters after his application to join in 1932 was refused. Kind, direct and encouraging, she continued to take a lively interest in his progress and as late as 1948 ventured up to London twice to see his autumn exhibition at Colnaghi's. They shared a mutual love not just of horses but more particularly of the circus and both had followed the tenting life, Seago as a young lad, Lucy as an older lady. Indeed, the circus presented Lucy with her most rewarding post-War challenge and it was to embrace it whole-heartedly that she finally relinquished the unequal struggle with her school.

Launching the Lifeboat. *Oil on canvas, 96in x 66in. Originally entitled* ***The Call from the Sea,*** *this composition had been suggested to Lucy by Edward Seago but, by 1937 when she started to paint it, the last horse-drawn lifeboat in Britain had been withdrawn from service.*

Sketch for ***Launching the Lifeboat.*** *Oil on board, 13in x 18in.*

Aristocrats. *Oil on canvas, 40in x 50in, 1928. The Hanoverian creams, including Royal, Cognac and Soda, were the pride of the Sanger stable.*

CHAPTER TEN

"Jakes and the Lady"

Barnet Fair *(Black Beauty, 1915)*

'Horses as Performers'

In July 1926, at short notice to her pupils but with a great sigh of relief, Lucy closed her school permanently and, attaching a caravan to 'Spitfire', her old Ford car, set off to follow the circus. She had gone down to Sanger's circus in search of material when it was visiting Watford and apparently the sight of one, old piece of worn harness had been enough. She saw such masses of beautiful, spontaneous subjects behind the scenes that she resolved there and then to accompany them on their journey. And so, chucking her responsibilities at last, she left Bushey behind.

Fred Elwell had been the first artist to travel with the show, in a gypsy caravan drawn by horses and George Sanger, ever a showman, was delighted to have another painter join their troupe. He was the third generation of his family involved in the circus, their fortunes founded by the brothers 'Lord' John and 'Lord' George Sanger over fifty years earlier. 'Lord' George had elevated himself to the peerage after a legal run-in with Buffalo Bill, the Honourable William Cody, and John Sanger, then running a rival show, had followed suit. Young George, John's grandson, had re-united the two families by marrying his cousin

---

Amidst the bustle of the horse fair Black Beauty discovered Jerry, the kindly, horsewise cab driver. Lucy was similarly impressed with the horsemastership of the circus company.

Stars at Leisure. *Oil on canvas, 24in x 30in, 1928-30. Lucy was fascinated at how quickly and efficiently the tenters swung into action erecting the canvas when a camp site was reached.*

Georgina, Lord George's grand-daughter. The tenting season ran from March until October and though Sanger's was a sizeable outfit they rarely stayed more than one night anywhere. For Lucy, the business of striking camp and moving on was an adventure:

> "What deep blue velvet nights spattered with lights on every side which disappear one by one, until sometime after midnight a silence falls on the great camp for an hour or so, then – what dawns! How lovely! as we wend our way to the next town through the pearl grey landscape so quiet, so fresh and the sun gets up and we put out our lamps and come clattering into the town which is still asleep behind drawn blinds."

Their pitch moved further out of the towns each year as land became scarcer. George Sanger would stand near the gateway, often narrow and awkward, of the chosen field and wave each loaded van to its designated place, the site of the Big Top having usually been staked out several days before. Lucy marvelled at

Comrades of Many Journeys. *Watercolour, 30in x 42in, 1928-29. The Sanger horses were not only performers but also helped transport the circus from town to town. Lucy's alternative title for this watercolour was* ***Transport Teams****.*

The Elephant Queen. *Pastel, 1929. Lucy, who rarely painted people, sketched both Mrs George Sanger Junior and Mrs Freeman in their striking costumes.*

the meticulous organisation which had the Big Top erected and the horse tents raised in three hours:

> "Instantly every man leaps from the wagons to his appointed place and work begins in earnest. There is no confusion, no asking of questions, the great king poles rise as if by magic, are made taut and firm, for on these two huge masts the acrobats depend for their lives. Up goes the giant weight of the canvas drawn to the top of each mast by a gang of tentmen to a monotonous chant of their own. Then comes the stretching of the width of the tent with hundreds of poles and cables strained to the

The Rosinback. *Canvas board, 20in x 24in, 1930. Lucy visited Sanger's winter quarters at Horley where the equestrian tricks were devised and perfected. Laura Knight exhibited a painting of 'The Trick Rider' at the RA in 1931 but her pictures, 'The Finishing Horse' and 'Allez-Oop', which related to this scene by Lucy, were not exhibited until 1951 and 1952.*

ground with tremendous labour of pile driving, five men with mallets to each post. The vast business of setting up the seating is going on inside like clockwork, and the great structure is complete…"

Only then was a communal breakfast served. The elephant men and horse keepers meanwhile put up the long lines of canvas for their charges who stood about resting after their journey and before the parade. Spoilt for a choice of subjects, Lucy tried not to get under people's feet while operations were in progress but the horse tents were a favourite resort:

"I love their rows of kind faces as they stand tied in the long horse tents. They are all known by name and spoken of as friends. The cream horses… are a great feature of this circus and are wonderfully trained. There is a long procession of them ranging from 'Royal' a great creature

Study for ***Autumn Gold.*** *Oil, 1933. The decline of horse transport restored Lucy's early interest in gypsies and now whenever they were in the locality she rushed out to paint them.*

> 17 hands high, down to quite little ponies, all with blue eyes and pink skins and chestnut-coloured tails, almost unique in shape and colour and now I believe almost unprocurable..."

These Hanoverian creams, formerly the prerogative of the monarch, shared a large square tent with a whole string of cream ponies of various sizes who kept a hopeful eye on Lucy's pocket. Their tent was built around a heavy wagon which served as manger and hay rack for the biggest horses and also prevented them from snapping at each other. Lucy watched and painted as they were brushed and prepared for the afternoon perfomance, their beautiful amber tails and manes combed and dressed with blue or scarlet plumes and trappings. Then, "with an attendant groom at each stately head they step forth like the aristocrats they are, to the entrance of the big tent where they meet their trainer and go through their parts."

Behind the Scenes. *Oil on board, 18in x 23in, 1928-30. Lucy's favourite sketching place was behind the scenes with the animals, unlike Laura Knight who preferred the ring and human interaction.*

Circus Pony Rider. *Watercolour, 9in x 14in. Watercolour notes caught the immediacy of the performance and applause.*

Lucy translated these moments into paintings, a large picture, 'Aristocrats', completed in 1928 depicting the horses on the way to the Big Top and another for George Sanger, showing them about to enter the ring. She painted 'Royal', who had been bought directly from the Royal stables, several times, and his companions 'Cognac' and 'Soda' were also captured in oil paint. After each act they would turn expectantly to their trainer, Alexander Hess, for their reward. Members of the Sanger family and the clowns, all accomplished equestrians themselves, took as much interest in the training as Hess and Lucy testified that there was no cruelty involved. She visited Sanger's winter quarters, Burstow Lodge at Horley in Surrey, and observed the daily, out of season, routine as tricks for the next summer were introduced and rehearsed endlessly in the practice ring, otherwise called 'the palace'. Horses which were to be danced on needed broad, fat backs and no sign of nerves as they were gradually accustomed to acrobats standing, pirouetting, tumbling on, off and round them. Lucy likewise remarked the gentle process by which a black mare was taught to jump through hoops, starting by walking through a bare hoop on the ground and graduating by slow stages to leaping through a hoop completely covered in paper.

Nevertheless, of the forty or fifty horses accompanying the circus, only a few were trained like this. The others, white, spotted, bay, dun, were draught horses which pulled the vans. Yet most, Lucy discovered, had some special gift so that

at a pinch they could understudy for one of the star performers. Inevitably she had a soft spot for these workaday beasts and was delighted to find that among the circus folk their doings were of absorbing interest. Their idiosyncracies were discussed daily, from old 'Lemon', a strange, independent, yellow mare who always roamed free because she was so sensible, to 'Tommy', a fat little mule no

Going Strong. *Pastel, 20in x 24in, 1933. One of a short series of racing pastels which Lucy undertook in the early thirties.*

bigger than a Shetland pony, who would not touch his food if there were oats in it but occasionally accepted a carrot. For one huge Canadian grey, however, very fat and strong, during all Lucy's travels they found no substitute. He made nothing of having five people on and off his back at once.

The elephants, Ida, Annie, Jenny and Tiny, had their idiosyncracies too. One, Lucy found, took delight in pushing people gently with one of her enormous forefeet, a habit which was turned into an effective act in the ring by putting a boxing glove on her. She also played football this way. Lucy was amused at the incongruity of the elephants grazing in English meadows, sweeping bundles of stinging nettles up with their trunks and pushing them sideways into their mouths.

Lucy clearly preferred the elephants to the wild cats and executed a large watercolour of them as a poster for the show. In those days, before television

Elephants and the Big Top. *Oil on canvas, 19¾in x 23¾in, 1928-30. Lucy painted a large watercolour of the elephants, Ida, Annie, Jenny and Tiny, as a poster for Sanger's in 1929.*

documentaries and safari parks, they were one of the main attractions in the parade advertising the circus' arrival in a town. Another feature of the Sanger's bill at this time, 'Dick Turpin's Ride to York', an equestrian stunt complete with coach and four, added a touch of drama to the parade as a masked highwayman galloped through the town on Black Bess to hold them up. Lucy's version of the circus' arrival at Ely in 1928, however, was typically low-key and behind-the-scenes. Entitled 'After a Hot Journey', her subject was horses bathing in the river and the canvas was reminiscent of Munnings' 'The Ford' (RA 1911).

Lucy fitted unobtrusively into the Sanger clan and in 1929 attended their annual dinner dance at the Criterion. Her travels with their circus over four or five years were remembered by Frank Foster, alias Dick Turpin.[33] Trained as a horseman and clown, Foster's unusual skill with horses acquired through Sanger's had led to his being excused the compulsory three-months riding school at Aldershot when he joined the cavalry in 1915. He was wooed away

33. Frank Foster, *Pink Coat, Spangles and Sawdust*, Stanley Paul & Co.

from Sangers at the end of the 1930 season by Bertram Mills who was setting up a tenting venture to complement his Christmas season at Olympia. As ringmaster, Foster encountered various other painters associated with circuses, Edward Seago, Steven Spurrier, Clifford Hall and Laura Knight, who had worked at Olympia. Laura Knight immersed herself in the activities of the human artistes so that her drawing books thronged with characters such as Togare, the lion tamer, Con Colleano, the tight rope-walker, and Whimsical Walker, the clown. She loved the audience arriving to envelop her, which was the point when Lucy usually retreated to her caravan, but while Laura Knight conveyed the gossipy excitement of circus life, her animals never quivered, sweated or smelt as Lucy's did. As if in reflection of their own personalities, Laura responded to the glitter and razzmatazz of the performance, Lucy to the discipline and teamwork which lay behind it.

The circus featured prominently in Lucy's exhibitions at the Arlington Gallery, the first in January 1934 shared with Albert Collings and some fellow members of the RI, the next in June and July 1938, a one-man show. Here circus paintings hung alongside a few racing and polo scenes, which had been rather unlikely subjects for Lucy until recently when her range became so curtailed. Lucy had visited both Goodwood and Cowdray Park in 1913 but, although she made vague plans to work there, it was not until the post-War period that she

Polo – The Great Game. *Oil on canvas, 38in x 48in, 1927. Mr de Monbrison commissioned Lucy to paint his polo ponies and she sketched games in progress at Ranelagh and the Hurlingham Club.*

***After a Hot Journey.** Oil on canvas, 24in x 30in, 1928. When they arrived in a new town the ponies had only a few hours rest before dressing up for the big parade.*

attempted any serious work. Meanwhile, in 1927, Mr de Monbrison commissioned studies of his polo ponies and Lucy sketched games in progress at Hurlingham and Ranelagh for a full scale composition entitled 'Polo – The Great Game'.

The polo pony studies and most of the racing pictures which she undertook during the thirties were executed in pastel, a medium which Lucy had used increasingly since the War. She had been elected a member of the Pastel Society and the Royal Institute of Painters in Watercolour in 1917 and both media had a distinct advantage over oil paint once she became a circus nomad. Speed of execution was a decisive factor, for it was no joke trying to store slow-drying oils in a corner of the tiny caravan which served as home and studio for weeks on end. For the same reason she also reduced the size of her pictures, working usually on a more portable scale. Gone were the days of the big picture case; now very often the back of someone else's caravan served as her easel for a few hours and at dawn they would all be on the move again.

In racing and polo, where horses supplied both sport and entertainment, their supremacy was unthreatened. Between the wars the circus provided another, albeit temporary, oasis where man's traditional dependence on the horse, which had been the inspiration for Lucy's labouring images, survived anachronistically because these animals could also double as performers. It was with sadness and some foreboding therefore that, as Frank Foster cranked her little car up for her at the end of her last season with Sangers, Lucy admitted that she was in bad shape and no longer had the stamina to follow the tenting life. Travelling with the circus had been a decisive bid for independence, reminiscent of her younger days, but it had taken tremendous energy and commitment. Edith's prolonged ill-health was sapping Lucy's strength too. Forced now into taking a back seat, it was only too easy for her to identify with the rising tide of redundant workhorses.

Throughout the thirties, news of gypsies camping in the local by-lanes or on the common sent her hurrying to paint them, precious glimpses of the

LORD JOHN
SANGER'S

Preliminary drawing for ***Sport of Imperial Rome****. Red chalk and gouache, 14in x 10in, 1931-32.*

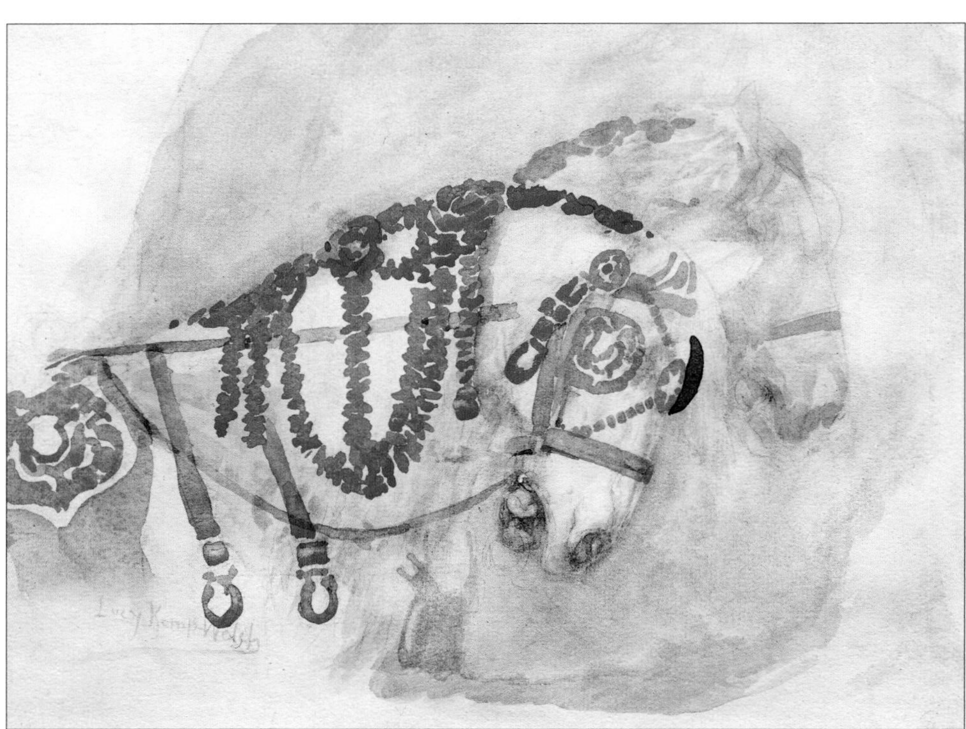

Circus Ponies. *Watercolour, 11in x 13½in. Watercolours and pastels could be stored more easily than oils in Lucy's tiny caravan when she travelled with Sanger's Circus.*

Sketch for ***A Holiday in Rome****. Pastel, c.1927. Lucy's depiction of a Roman chariot race may have been inspired by her current interest in both circuses and racing.*

Summer Dawn*. Watercolour, 12in x 14in, 1928. Lucy loved trundling through the summer dawn with the travelling circus.*

vanishing horse-drawn world of her childhood. She envied them living so close to nature, so free of impediments, and was fascinated by their language and traditions. Indeed, travelling folk and their horses had been the spark behind her first Academy painting, 'Gypsy Horse Drovers', but, with the outbreak of the Second World War, such glimpses became even rarer, the mechanised world more destructive.

This time, villagers did not stand in Bushey High Street watching the Blitz on London; they suffered it too. Indeed on 7 October 1940 a bomb landed right opposite Kingsley, killing two soldiers, injuring twelve civilians and destroying the lychgate which had been erected as a memorial after the First World War. Although Lucy and Edith were unhurt, Kingsley itself was badly damaged with the roof and upstairs rooms in tatters and the windows shattered.

For horses, war once more provided a brief revival of fortune as petrol rationing and the Land Army swung into action but for Lucy there was no reprieve. On 3 November 1941, Edith died of cancer and, although Marguerite Frobisher came to live at Kingsley, Lucy became

The Gypsy Camp. *Oil on board, 9¾in x 13¾in, c.1951.*

increasingly reclusive. Her eyesight had begun to fail and most of the pictures which she still submitted to the Academy and other societies had been completed years before. Although she designed and oversaw the building of an ambitious replica Elizabethan Gateway for Bushey's Coronation celebrations in 1953, her last exhibit at the Royal Academy was 'Harvest of the Beech Woods' in 1949.

A Little More and How Much It Is. *Pastel, 18in x 24in, 1933. Lucy had planned a racing picture in 1913, visiting Goodwood to make sketches, but it was not until after the War that she took up the subject again.*

In January that year, the Royal Academy had mounted an exhibition of the Chantrey Bequest collection and both Lucy's paintings were on show. Fifty years melted like snow as 'Colt Hunting in the New Forest' hung on the line again at Burlington House. Lucy, tiny, honest, indomitable as ever, could not fail to be delighted, yet Fate had played some curious tricks on her in that time. Her old friend Alfred Munnings for instance, whom she could have painted into a cocked hat in 1897, was now the Academy's President and knighted too. A tall, convivial, outspoken man, he was, like Laura Knight, a survivor, a natural performer. Curiously too, it was only as performers that race-horses, hunters, show-jumpers and ceremonial cavalry horses now survived from among their hard-working colleagues, a complete reversal of the status quo ante.

For Lucy, however, art and horses were not about performance or after-dinner speeches; they were about living and breathing. "Painting horses", she wrote as an old lady, "is to me the breath of life", a truth witnessed nowhere more amply than in her rendering of *Black Beauty*, whose virtuosity stands unchallenged to this day.

CHAPTER ELEVEN

"The Golden Rule"

It Was Ginger *(Black Beauty, 1915)*

'Horses as People'

Lucy's popular success as a painter was based almost entirely on her empathy with horses and developed out of the companionship and freedom they had provided for her as a child. It was not just that she understood horse character but that she read and, as a painter, communicated horse body language intuitively, with a sparkling highlight or a touch of shadow, the pencil quiver of a muscle here, the oily toss of a mane there. Moreover, uniquely among horse painters, this was her primary purpose, for she placed a higher priority on conveying the character and emotions of horses themselves, than on depicting them in relation to man. For others they might represent sport, class, breeding, athleticism, property, power or rural life. For Lucy essentially they stood for nothing but themselves. In short, she treated them like people.

There was nothing sentimental or anthropomorphic in this; it was simply a matter of the value she invested in them as individuals, of her seeing their vocations from the equine point of view. Her skill was in achieving the exact balance of light and air, life and drama, tenderness and strength to convince

Lucy's illustration for Chapter XL capitalised on the priority she had always given to conveying the character and emotions of horses themselves rather than on their relationship to man.

Black Prince immortalised as Black Beauty.

others that her angle was just. As a tiro she had managed this by instinct, picking on subjects which coincidentally mirrored her own emotional circumstances. It was not until 1902, however, that she realised consciously that for her not only must the driving force be sincerity or truthfulness, but that, incredibly, truth involved a balancing act. The more effectively she manipulated the interaction in the composition between subject, lighting, colour, movement, mass and so on, the more truthful her work would be seen to be. From that moment she was in complete command of her paintings and her reputation soared.

By early 1915, when J.M. Dent commissioned her to illustrate *Black Beauty*,

My Early Home. *Pen and ink over pencil, 8in x 8in, 1915, illustration from* Black Beauty. *The galloping colts in the headpiece to Chapter I and the endpapers echoed* ***Colt Hunting*** *and* ***The Joy of Life*** *but the rolling clouds also signalled the further evolution of the freedom and restraint themes in Lucy's post-war work.*

Lucy with Black Prince, her model for Black Beauty.

Lucy was at the height of her powers. Her earlier illustrative work, particularly with regard to Whyte Melville's novels, had won some praise in the press but was not exceptional. It had been undertaken as a stopgap when she was trying to find her own voice and attempting various narrative pictures herself. It was clear that her gift lay in interpreting her own, not someone else's, script. Yet as she had gradually established her own vision and moved away from formal, external narrative, there was a sense in which her paintings became more dramatic, like the internal monologues of Robert Browning, her favourite poet. They revealed, unconsciously perhaps, action within characters as much as characters in action.

Lucy's headpiece for Chapter XLIII drew on her many previous studies of carthorses like ***Farm Hand.***

Farm Hand. *Oil on canvas laid down, 12in x 10in.*

Added to the already impressive list of qualifications, her gender, attitude, horsesmanship, and experience, which fitted Lucy to the task of bodying forth *Black Beauty*, was the unquantifiable, personal value of Black Prince. Indeed the commission may well have arisen out of 'The Riders' (RA 1911) in whose creation Black Prince had played such a significant role. As Baden-Powell remarked, Lucy's book immortalised Black Prince and transformed a temperamental charger into a children's hero. In any event, just as Anna Sewell seems to have had before her as a model her brother's horse, Black Bess,[34] so Lucy's rapport with Black Prince rooted her illustrations in a defined personality and sparked an emotional charge.

Lucy scheduled likely illustrations on her well-thumbed copy of *Black Beauty*, marking relevant incidents in the text with pencil and potential locations for colour plates with small red circles. Now beginning to disintegrate, the book

34. 'The Annotated Black Beauty' with introduction and annotations by Ellen B. Wells and Anne Grimshaw (1989) p.xii.

It Was An Anxious Time *(Black Beauty, 1915). Oil. It is not Lucy's skill as an illustrator so much as her intuitive empathy with horses, evidenced here in Black Beauty's anxiety over who would be his future owner, which explains the extraordinary success of her version of the book.*

The headpiece to Chapter VII. Lucy's designs for this and several other chapters originally incorporated the chapter title. Most were later dropped by the publishers although the edges of the scroll here remain.

was the Jarrold's first edition belonging to her father and in itself a memento of her childhood. She carefully annotated the head and tailpieces for every chapter, 'head of Merrylegs with convolvulus border' (Chapter IX) or 'the cabmen look at a new horse' (Chapter XXXIII). On occasions, she scratched an idea out or moved it on to another chapter, while once or twice she roughed out a sketch on the page in pencil. These are identifiable now as finished drawings in the Dent's edition and suggest that Lucy had a clear concept from

Headpiece to Chapter XXXII, 'A Horse Fair'. Lucy's earliest composition, ***Gypsy Horse Drovers****, had dealt with animals on their way to the Barnet Horse Fair, which itself featured in her* Black Beauty*. However her illustrations also looked forward, uncannily, to the time when she would join a travelling circus.*

Headpiece for Chapter XI. For borders and drawn titles Lucy was indebted to the Aesthetic Movement.

the start of how she envisaged her *Black Beauty*.

All the reference material she needed was at her fingertips for, like Black Beauty himself, she had encountered all sorts of horses and people in the course of her career. She had been present at births and sometimes too at tragic deaths. One of her most vivid memories as a teenager, for instance, was running to fetch her sketchbook to draw a horse which had fallen dead between the shafts of a cart just as Ginger did. This may have been the inspiration also behind 'Down!' (Chapter XLVII), one of the many instances in which Black Beauty's memories prompted Lucy's. Indeed, the parallels with her earlier paintings are not hard to find. 'New Year's Eve' (Chapter XLV) suggests 'The Village Street',

Headpieces to Chapters XV and XXVII.

It Was a Nasty Thing (Black Beauty, *1915). One of the first illustrations Lucy produced for the 1915 Limited Edition of* Black Beauty, *this drawing was executed in pen and ink with watercolour washes but was used in black and white in some cheaper editions.*

The Start*. Pastel, 9in x 23in, 1933. The old ostler in* Black Beauty, *an ex-jockey, had broken his knee riding at Goodwood. Lucy was able to use her knowledge of the racecourse there when she was illustrating the book.*

***Ambling Home**. Oil on canvas, 18in x 24in, summer 1913. Lucy's working title for this picture, painted at Cocking in Sussex, was **The Mill Dam**. A preparatory study for her 1914 Royal Academy exhibit, **The Glory of the Day**, it also provided the setting for Lucy's illustration in Chapter III, **It was a Nasty Thing**.*

'Now, Auster, Do Your Best' (Chapter XXIV) suggests 'The Riders'. 'The Brick Cart' (Chapter XX) relates to 'The Laggard' and timber-hauling studies, while 'It Was a Nasty Thing' (Chapter III) recalls 'Ambling Home' and other scenes round the mill dam at Cocking. 'Mixed Company at a Race Meeting' (RA 1905), which started life originally as the large version of 'Sons of the City', was reincarnated in 'It Was An Anxious Time' (Chapter XLVIII). Likewise, 'The Morning of Balaclava' (Chapter XXXIV) had its origins in Lucy's Boer War studies, with the black and white tailpiece to that chapter, 'Without Master or Friend', harking back to 'The Morning'. Meanwhile, 'The Morning' also re-

appears in 'I Stood There and Listened' (Chapter XXV) when Black Beauty waits for help in the night beside Reuben Smith's body.

That Lucy had written her own script for these scenes in earlier paintings enhanced rather than detracted from their immediacy. Active participation in her subjects had always been of paramount importance to her. The line drawings similarly called upon her past, most temptingly the endpapers of charging colts which seem to have galloped straight out of 'The Joy of Life'. This type of quotation occurs throughout the book, with the stag's head referring back to 'For Life', the pair of cart-horses to 'The Night Cometh', the cavalry horses to 'Sons of the City', the foals at the fence to 'What Comes?' Some of the views are easily identifiable too, the race course being Goodwood and Earlshall being Moor Park near Bushey.

Not all the references are retrospective, however. The bridge Lucy depicted in Chapter XII provided the setting later for 'The River Way' and 'Across The Ford'

Headpiece for Chapter XXII. Lucy modelled Earlshall loosely on the Palladian mansion, Moor Park, near Rickmansworth in Hertfordshire.

too, although these paintings were not completed until about 1934. Some of the coloured plates hold similar glimpses of the future. Thus 'Barnet Fair' (Chapter XXXII) with its references to horse dealers and fairs looks both backward to Lucy's gypsy drovers and forward to her future with the circus. The frontispiece, 'She Chose Me for Her Horse', also straddles time, Lady Anne in her riding habit beside Black Auster resembling the heroine of 'The Riders' although closer in age to 'Young April'. This watercolour also predicts 'Breeze and Broad Spaces', Lucy's portrait of Elizabeth Usborne and her Arab, which would not be painted until 1926.

The model for Lady Anne in the 1915 frontispiece was Dent's daughter, Muriel, who sat for Lucy at Bushey on 3 and 6 August. This, like 'Barnet Fair', was among the last coloured drawings completed. 'My Mother and I' on the other hand, which echoed Lucy's mother-foal sequence of 1904-07 was one of the first illustrations she undertook, indicating presumably that it was a theme with which she immediately identified. In 1918 this sketch was translated into an oil painting on board, probably as a commission. Entitled 'The Promise of Spring' it found its way eventually into Philip Dennison's collection in Canada.

In spite of the planning, the actual process of illustration started slowly,

They Both Flew to her Head *(*Black Beauty, *1915). Lucy was in sympathy with Black Beauty's didactic origins, highlighted particularly during this incident at Earlshall when Ginger reacts violently to the over-tight bearing rein.*

Down! (Black Beauty, *1915). Lucy recalled how as a child she had seen a horse fall dead between the shafts and ran immediately to fetch her drawing book.*

Breeze and Broad Spaces – Elizabeth Usborne and her Arab Horse. *Watercolour, 24in. x 30in, 1926. This portrait commission looked back to Lucy's earlier frontispiece for* Black Beauty *which had featured Muriel Dent.*

The Promise of Spring. *Oil on board, 17½in x 14in, 1918. This oil, based on Lucy's illustration for the first chapter of Black Beauty, was acquired by Philip Denison after the War.*

Medallion for the Society of Animal Painters, 1914. Lucy's design of a winged Pegasus as an emblem resembled the blocked and gilded roundel incorporating the heads of Ginger and Black Beauty which she produced the following year for the front cover of the Limited Edition of Black Beauty.

impeded possibly by the accident in which Lucy damaged her knee. She embarked on the first illustration on 2 February 1915, an oil on canvas to accompany Chapter XVI, 'Fire!'. 'My Mother and I', an oil on grey paper, was finished on 15 February and 'In The Orchard' and 'It Was A Nasty Thing', both pen and ink drawings with colour washes, followed within a fortnight. The line drawing of galloping colts, which was intended for the endpapers of the limited edition but which also served as the printed cover for the popular edition, was completed in early March and a segment of this was used as the headpiece for Chapter I, 'My Early Home'. Preparations for the Royal Academy Summer Exhibition may have proved a further distraction for, apart from two line drawings, Lucy did little more towards the project until May. She resumed work with 'The Hunt' but by the time Dent himself came down to Bushey with his daughter on 25 June, to see how the illustrations were progressing, Lucy had still finished only a dozen drawings at the most.

Whatever transpired at that meeting, from then on Lucy worked extremely quickly, dispatching packets of three or four drawings to Dent's on an almost weekly basis, so that by mid-August they had received all thirty colour illustrations. Over the next six weeks, while holidaying in Sussex, Lucy concentrated on the black and white chapter headings and tailpieces, while

Headpiece for Chapter XII, 'A Stormy Day'. This plank bridge later featured in ***Across the Ford*** *and* ***The River Way***.

Headpiece to Chapter XXXIV. ***An Old War Horse*** *retained elements of Lucy's Boer War painting,* ***Sons of the City*** *(page 59).*

Dent's sent colour proofs back and forth for corrections. By October the task was completed and all that remained in November was for her to sign the fly sheets for the de luxe and limited editions.

The coloured illustrations were completed in a mixture of media, two being oil on canvas, several others being oil on grey paper, and the majority being in a variety of watercolour techniques. Whether this arrangement was discussed with Dent's or was Lucy's decision is not known, but it seems likely that 'Fire!' was executed on canvas for practical reasons, to achieve the density of colour required in printing. Oils on grey paper, such as 'My Mother and I' or 'If Only I Could Get Him Off', were much sketchier, leaving areas of the paper free in contrast to the more finished watercolours. Occasionally Lucy highlighted both oils and watercolours with gouache. A further group of coloured illustrations, highly detailed pen and ink drawings washed over with watercolour, had a more

Headpieces to Chapters XLII and XLV. Lucy's uncharacteristically sophisticated use of space in her urban illustrations suggests the work of contemporary graphic artists and illustrators such as the Beggarstaff Brothers, William Heath Robinson or Aubrey Beardsley. In the city scenes Lucy focused attention deliberately on the streets and pavements which took such a toll on cab horses' health and were the antithesis of open skies.

***Across the Ford**. Oil on board, 12in x 18in, c.1934. An oil sketch for **The River Way** which Lucy painted on commission for a friend's library.*

precise effect than was characteristic of Lucy. However, as half a dozen of these were later reproduced as the full page black and white illustrations in the reduced 1921 edition of *Black Beauty*, presumably Dent's had pre-selected and commissioned them with this adaptability in mind. Of the thirty coloured plates in the 1915 Limited Edition, only twelve were included in the 1915 Popular Edition but these represented a variety of techniques and media.

Lucy had discussed the business aspects of the commission with Arthur Rackham and he may have given her some guidance too concerning the pen, ink and watercolour illustrations of which he was a master. In some places Lucy even adopted his practice of framing the signature in a scroll. The influence of other contemporary illustrators was evident elsewhere, more particularly in the black and white drawings rather than the coloured illustrations which evolved directly out of her style as an independent painter. The use of exaggerated space for

Heat of Noon. *Oil on canvas, 18in x 24in, 1933. Lucy had made use earlier of the way horses sharing a field often gather together in the shade as if conversationally in the headpiece to Chapter X,* ***A Talk in the Orchard*** *(left).*

Lucy's Black Beauty *is studded with country scenes, some of which have little or no reference to horses, but all of which emphasise the fresh air, open sky and rolling hills which are the natural environment for horses, wild or tame.*

instance, in the London chapter headings, pushing action to the margins, suggests the work of William Heath Robinson, the Beggarstaff Brothers or Aubrey Beardsley. Originally derived from Japanese prints and adopted by the Impressionists, this had become a fashionable convention among graphic artists and Lucy may have employed it tongue in cheek to convey urban sophistication. In many ways it was a device alien to Lucy and she did not exploit the interplay of black-white mass-space as creatively as her exemplars. On the other hand, it amply illustrated the strangeness of this new society to a horse bred in the country. The single-minded focus of these London scenes on the streets and pavements beneath Black Beauty's hooves contrasted deliberately with the emphasis on wind and sky in the country pieces, and intensified the conflict between the drudgery of his existence as a broken-down cab-horse and the freedom of his happy youth.

For her borders and drawn titles, Lucy was equally indebted to the Aesthetic Movement which had elevated book illustration into a separate art form by the turn of the nineteenth century. Nonetheless, because of their artifice, Lucy's panels of fruit or trees, although excellent decorations in the *Studio Magazine* tradition, had no virtue for her as drawings outside the confines of the book. This is perhaps what most distinguishes Lucy from other illustrators, such as Arthur Rackham, Edmund Dulac or William Heath Robinson, whose art grew out of fantasy. The best illustrators do not just interpret, they amplify a narrative, in some cases becoming inseparable from it. Thus E.H. Shepherd will eternally be associated with *Winnie the Pooh* and Phiz with Dickens. Occasionally, the artist's imagination even outstrips the text and such books are prized simply for their exquisite drawings. The one quality all gifted illustrators seem to have in common, however, is whimsy.

Nothing could be further from Lucy's attitude to art than whimsy, yet she was undeniably *Black Beauty*'s most successful illustrator, her drawings illuminating and enriching the story. That the book has proved to be the best selling children's illustrated book ever and has endured for so long must surely be a publishing fluke, the exception which proves the rule for certainly, measured against Rackham or Dulac, Lucy was no illustrator. She was by instinct and training a painter and dealt in reality. And that, strangely enough, explains the extraordinary success of her *Black Beauty.*

***Something in the Wind**. Watercolour, 21in x 27in, 1937. During the thirties Lucy focused increasingly on imagery which extolled the naturally free spirit of even working horses.*

CHAPTER TWELVE

"The Autobiography of a Horse Painter"

It Fell Right Across the Road *(Black Beauty, 1915)*

There could not have been a more pertinent time for a horse painter, particularly a woman, to have worked than the close of the nineteenth century. For horses as much as for women, the world was in transition and Lucy, albeit inadvertently, had taken advantage of it. After centuries in which the fundamental role both played in western civilisation had been scarcely recognised, women were on the brink of asserting themselves, horses on the brink of decline. Yet, although she seemed to be forging her way ahead independently, success accrued to Lucy almost accidentally and she never acquired the skills to pursue her own advantage ruthlessly. By the twenties Lucy, marooned in the unfashionable world of animal painting, found her constituency contracting while other women artists saw theirs expand. She seemed destined, ironically, to share the fate of her horses.

Nevertheless, as a painter of horses rather than horseflesh, Lucy has never been rivalled. She was no ordinary horse-painter. Where most of her male contemporaries, Munnings for instance, Cecil Aldin, Lionel Edwards, were painting from a man-centred viewpoint, Lucy's best work was always horse-

---

Rainy tracks, reminiscent of *The Village Street* (page 69), lead the reader into a dramatic moment in the tale.

centred. It was a perspective which, though she would probably have scorned the idea, undoubtedly owed much to her being a woman. Although psychologists claim women see relationships in terms of intimacy and men see them in terms of power, where horses are concerned women's emotions may be more ambivalent, the intimacy itself a means of achieving strength. This was particularly true at the turn of the century. In any event, this ambivalent relationship added dramatically to the tension and attraction of Lucy's painting. It also corresponded neatly with Anna Sewell's scenario, a male horse narrating a lady's story.

For its part, *Black Beauty* is no ordinary children's story. Far removed from fairytale, it is an equine *Pilgrim's Progress*, appealing equally to those who love or know nothing about horses. In this it resembles Lucy's paintings closely and for Lucy its plain-speaking style was a virtue. She could create the illustrations for the text in the same way as she painted her other pictures, out of the fabric of her own life. Thus, where a part of the story was largely fiction, Lucy supplied the facts and where passages were didactic she supplied the sympathy. As in her other paintings, it was all a question of sincerity, balancing strength and intimacy, fact and feeling.

The feelings Lucy presented in her paintings, however, were far more personal than she realised. Just as particular groups of pictures seem to be associated with various phases in her life, so certain topics, freedom and restraint, maternity and loss, communication and control, recur constantly under different guises, mingling, mutating, evolving. Thus the few hard facts in her diaries are fleshed out by the themes highlighted in the paintings, where every brushstroke has a purpose.

***Ploughing on the South Downs**. Watercolour, 6in x 9in. During the thirties Lucy became fluent at suggesting tiny nuances of weather and atmosphere.*

Horse's Head in the Sky. *Watercolour, 8¼in x 12¼in. Her prowess as a horsewoman and artist effectively empancipated Lucy ahead of her times, but success had accrued to her almost accidentally.*

However reticent she might have been with words, it was impossible for Lucy to suppress her feelings when she was painting. Indeed, although she implied to Seago that feelings were at the root of the "impulse to paint", she confessed quite frankly elsewhere that she did not know where the emotions she painted came from:

> "Now as to the actual painting of animals – it is not the fondness for the animal which causes a man fully equipped with the power to paint – to forsake all else for this branch of art – but deep at the heart of him is that something which dictates that he shall do this, that he shall wait and watch with patience infinite for this movement, or that appearance, shall obscure with that devotion to the subject all fear and hardship and will go through anything for the sake of attaining that one scrap of knowledge – and all this before he can paint."

Even in choosing her subjects, particularly before the First World War when possibilities were plentiful, Lucy was declaring her emotional hand and her range of subjects reflected her affections, hopes and fears. Although she believed in hard work and Christian values, throughout her life she yearned for freedom.

Burnt Out Fires. *Oil on canvas, 48in x 72in. Exhibited at the Royal Academy, 1927, repainted entirely, 1932. End-of-the-day scenes had appealed to Lucy from as early as* ***The Afterglow*** *in 1898 and this painting provided a poetic resolution of the theme, duty well done being its own reward.*

Horse's Head Against the Skyline. *Oil on canvas, 7½in x 8½in, c.1931-37. Lucy's horse paintings differed fundamentally from those of contemporaries such as Sir Alfred Munnings because her viewpoint was always horse, rather than man, centred.*

Mare and Foal at the County Show. *Oil on panel, 18in x 23in, c.1930-34. It was unusual for Lucy to paint the heavy horses she loved in so formal a pose but this mare and foal may have been connected with an American commission entitled* ***My Only Son***.

She plunged into new areas, riding with the Agisters, labouring with the timber-haulers, training with the remounts, travelling with the circus, painting on a huge scale, all silent declarations that she would not be impeded by her gender or her size. To some extent her determination prevailed and yet in the final analysis she was not selfish enough to be really successful. She was shackled in turn by social convention, the ill-health of family and friends, the needs of the school, male chauvinism, age, but above all by her own highly developed sense of duty. Therein lies her affection for the patient, labouring shire, her indifference to the highly-strung racehorse.

The vigour of her compositions, the vitality of her brushwork, widely admired as characteristics of her paintings, derived similarly from the horses expressing not just facets of real experience but more importantly her feelings about those experiences. Hence their energy is her energy, their youth her youth, their toil her toil, their joy her joy, and so on. By extension, therefore, Black Beauty's emotions too could be said to relate directly to Lucy's, particularly as she used Black Prince, whose arrival at Bushey was associated

Lucy, with Podger beside her, painting ***An Idle Day*** *in 1902.*

with a very sensitive phase in her life, as her model. Invariably her most successful paintings were those in which she had some empathy with the subject. Thus her youthful colt-hunting pictures reflected the loss of her parents and the excitement and fear of her new-found liberty. Once these feelings were resolved her work lost direction and it was not until she encountered Kim that her paintings once again took on a life of their own.

Above. ***Circus Ponies in the Shade of an Awning***. *Canvas laid down, 12in x 18in, c.1928-30. The circus provided Lucy with a safe haven where horses were still an essential part of the culture, although they had fallen into decline elsewhere.*

Left. ***Mist on the Fells***. *Oil, 16in x 19in, c.1932.*

Opposite. *Preparatory Study for* ***The Waterway***. *Oil, 23in x 20in, 1913. Lucy's affection for working horses may have lain in her own, similarly patient, application to duty.*

Head of a Rearing Horse. *Charcoal, 10¼in x 10¼in. A study for Lucy's 1917 Royal Academy painting* ***Forward the Guns.***

Interestingly however, the most atmospheric drawings in the text of *Black Beauty*, the harvest, hunt and windswept landscapes which top and tail various chapters, hardly feature horses at all. Although they demonstrate Lucy's love and familiarity with country pursuits, their purpose as they recur throughout the text is more than incidental. They carry Black Beauty's memories of joy and liberty with them through the text like a leitmotiv, subtly corroborating his gradual decline and lost aspirations. Moreover the subliminal, emotional current they propel through the text is probably that which corresponds most closely to Lucy's own state of mind in 1915.

Black Beauty provided the ideal vehicle for Lucy's further exploration of the freedom-restraint themes with which she had been playing since the earliest colt-hunting scenes. The windswept pen and ink drawings she created for the book stood mid-way between the recent, complicated emotions of 'The

Wild Horses (Black Beauty, *1915). Lucy's design for the endpapers of the limited edition touched closely upon her private feelings, particularly the yearning for freedom which was first expressed in* ***Gypsy Horse Drovers*** *and* ***Colt Hunting*** *and which went on to become a driving force behind her work.*

Homewards. *Charcoal, 9½in x 11½in. Dating from between the wars, this drawing shows how Lucy understood the paradox of the horse, the instincts which both bade him to be free and tied him into his landscape.*

Riders' and the liberated breeze pictures of the thirties. Identifying with Black Beauty's situation, Lucy projected feelings for him which were already potentially real for her. It was not premonition, simply a subconscious acceptance of the inevitable outcome for her of the continuing conflict between freedom and duty. For children then these drawings express the call of

***Polar Bears on the Ice Floe**. Oil on canvas, 16in x 20in, 1908. This is probably the painting entitled **Combat** which was commissioned from Lucy by Harold Ellis in May 1907. It was painted at London Zoo.*

***Cockerels**. Pastel, 15in x 21in, c.1945-50. An almost Japanese-style drawing which depicts Lucy's pet cockerel Tenpence in multiple poses.*

the wild; for adults, regret at vanishing youth and opportunity.

And so it was for Lucy. Travelling with the circus was a last attempt to throw over the traces. The publication of *Black Beauty* had been a watershed for her and, in spite of its popular reception, marked the turning point in her career. As she completed her assignment for Dent's, national events were beginning to overtake her, and her own 'Hard Times' lay ahead. At the outset of the First World War Lucy's *Black Beauty* chronicled an era which had been real for her but was already as romantic as history for many of her readers. With twenty productive years behind her and twenty ahead, she was still only half-way through her working life but for those who remember her as 'the lady who painted Black Beauty' the clock stopped here. She was perhaps the victim of her own youthful success. If she had not achieved so much so young she would probably have left Bushey to study elsewhere, found other opportunities and avoided later disappointments. On the other hand, had she done so, or had she married, she may never have needed to paint horses at all.

The extent of the book's success was unexpected. Ironically, just as Anna Sewell sold the text of *Black Beauty* outright to Jarrolds for £30, so Lucy sold her drawings to Dent's for £400. Neither of them received any further royalties. Dent recognised that the tone and purpose of Anna Sewell's book corresponded specifically to Lucy's attitude and experience. There was no other story, even *The Children of the New Forest*, with which Lucy could so readily have identified and this no doubt explains why she did not pursue illustration further. For Dent's and for Lucy it was a commission made in heaven and of its nature unrepeatable.

Lucy was then at the height of her powers, confident at last of her own ability and the reception her work would receive. Although the illustrations were only shadows of the vigorous, life-size oil paintings which had established her in the front rank of contemporary woman painters, as a group none the less they spoke of the intimate feelings which shaped her life and work. Translated into small-scale drawings, Lucy's experiences became a commentary more poignant than any personal diary. In many ways, too, they explain the lasting appeal of her *Black Beauty,* for she was painting the autobiography of an indomitable horse painter as much as the autobiography of a horse.

BIBLIOGRAPHY

Aldin, Cecil, *Time I Was Dead*, Eyre and Spottiswoode, 1934.
The Marquess of Anglesey, *A History of the British Cavalry*, Vols 4 & 5, Leo Cooper in association with Secker & Warburg 1986.

Cockcroft, Barry, *Princes of the Plough*.
Condell, Diana and Liddiard, Jean, *Working for Victory?* Routledge & Kegan Paul, 1987.

Edwards, Elwyn Hartley, *Horses: Their Role in the History of Man*, Channel 4/Scottish Television, 1987.

Flagg, James Montgomery, *Roses and Buckshot*.
Foster, Frank, *Pink Coat, Spangles and Sawdust*, Stanley Paul & Co.

Gillett, Paula, *The Victorian Painter's World*, Alan Sutton, 1990.

Heiney, Paul, *Pulling Punches*, Methuen, 1988.

Herkomer, Hubert von, *My School and My Gospel.*

Jeal, Tim, *Baden-Powell*, Hutchinson.

Longman, Grant, *The Herkomer Art School 1883-1900* and *The Herkomer Art Schoola and Subsequent Developments 1901-1908.*

Lukens, John, *The Sanger Story*, Hodder and Stoughton.

Frank Foster. Pink Coat, Spangles and Sawdust. Stanley Paul & Co.

Saxon Mills, J., *Life and Letters of Sir Hubert Herkomer*, Hutchinson & Co., 1923.

Nunn, Patricia Gerrish, *Victorian Women Artists*, The Women's Press, 1987.

Sewell, Ann, *Black Beauty*, Jarrold & Sons, 1877.

Street, Sean (ed.), *A Remembered Land*, Michael Joseph, 1994.

Wells, Ellen B. and Grimshaw, Anne (eds.), *The Annotated Black Beauty*, J.A. Allen, 1989.

PAINTINGS EXHIBITED OR SUBMITTED BY LUCY KEMP-WELCH TO THE ROYAL ACADEMY SUMMER EXHIBITIONS

The annual Summer Exhibition at the Royal Academy was the pivot around which Lucy planned her painting year and until the twenties at least it provided the major public showcase for her work. The following list has been compiled using her records:

1895	610	Gypsy Horse Drovers
1896	457	Foam Horses
	957	Summer Drought in the New Forest
1897	346	Colt Hunting in the New Forest *(£525 Chantrey Bequest Purchase)*
1898	570	'To Arms!' Early Morning in the Camp of the Duke of York's Army Before the Battle of the Roses at St Albans *(£1,000)*
1899	585	Harvesters
1900	427	Horses Bathing in the Sea
1901	417	'In Sight!' Lord Dundonald's Dash on Ladysmith *(£1,000)*
1902	233	The Morning *(£500)*
	264	Ploughing on the South Coast *(£800)*
1903	98	Sons of the City
	283	The Village Street *(£400)*
	356	The Incoming Tide *(£300)*
1904	330	Timber Hauling in the New Forest *(1,000 gns)*
1905	455	Mixed Company at a Race Meeting
	863	The Salmon Pool *(Watercolour)*
1906	356	The Joy of Life
	925	Horse Drovers *(Watercolour 60 gns)*
1907	336	The Laggard *(£400)*
	371	The Morning of the Year *(£300)*
1908	918	For Life
1909	516	What Comes?
	754	The Labour of the Forest *(Watercolour 70 gns)*
	Rejected	*Reprieve*
1910	117	Young April
	871	Sundown *(Watercolour)*
1911	722	The Riders *(£1,000)*
1912	462	The Passing Train *(£400)*
1913	922	The Return from the Fields *(£630)*
1914	108	The Glory of the Day/The Mill Pond *(£200)*
	606	The Waterway
1915	132	Ponte Sta. Trinita, Florence
	468	A Year Ago

1916	365	A Fold on the Downs
	688	The Morning Mist
1917	706	'Forward the Guns!' *(£800 Chantrey Bequest Purchase)*
1918	332	Big Guns Up to The Front *(£1,000)*
1919	186	Silks and Satins, Goodwood
	212	The Seaward Fields of Devon
1920	178	The Straw Ride, Russley Park Remount Depot *(£1,000)*
	435	The Enchanted Shore
1921	*Not hung*	*Market Night*
1922	*Not hung*	*Feeding the Multitude*
1923	198	The Woodman's Fire
	Not hung	*Log Hauling*
1924	399	Winter's White Silence
1925	402	Wanderers in Waste Places
1926	363	Hill Folk – Welsh Mountain Ponies Coming in to the Town over Brecon Bridge
	530	On the South Downs: Mrs Vyvyan Clark on her Grey Arab *(£100)*
1927	432	Burnt-Out Fires
1928	*Not hung*	*Polo – The Great Game*
1929	28	Timber Coming Down the Mountain in Wales
	209	O Shepherd of the Hills *(£200)*
1930	582	The Evening Camp
1931	*Not hung*	*Timber Run in the Welsh Hills*
1932	305	Timber Run in the Welsh Hills
1933	410	Hush of the Winter Ways
1934	346	A Moment's Rest *(£60)*
	635	Autumn Gold
1935	418	The Crest of the Downs *(£160)*
	639	Leisure in the Horse Tents
1936	*Not hung*	*Behind the Scenes*
	Not hung	*'Summer is A Cumin' In'*
1937	551	The Lumber Team
1938	581	A Shadow from the Heat
	Not hung	*The Forest Stream – Balmer's Lawn*
1939	*Not hung*	*A Call from the Sea*
1940	*Rejected*	*The Happy Autumn Fields*
1941	438	Horse Tents
	442	The River Meadow
1942	*Rejected*	*The Early Arrival (Travellers in the Night)*
1944	640	Ponte Vecchio, Florence
	Rejected	*The Travelling Circus*
1945	*Not hung*	*Behind the Scenes*
1948	*Not hung*	*At The Going Down of the Sun*
1949	369	Harvest of the Beech Woods

PAINTINGS BY LUCY KEMP-WELCH IN PUBLIC GALLERIES

Grundy Art Gallery, BLACKPOOL	The Waterway
Russell-Cotes Gallery, BOURNEMOUTH	Gypsy Horse Drovers Foam Horses Toilers Sport of Imperial Rome Autumn Gold Study for Gypsy Horse Drovers Pencil Drawing of a Horse's Head
BRISTOL Museums and Art Gallery	Timber Hauling in the New Forest
BURY Art Gallery and Museum	Watercolour sketch of Black Horse's Head
BUSHEY Museum and Art Gallery	Elephant Queen Barnet Fair Now Auster Do Your Best The Jubilee Arch, Bushey Bushey Church and Pond Collection of Drawings and Pastels Unfinished oil paintings
National Museum of Wales, CARDIFF	Big Guns Up To The Front
Royal Albert Memorial Museum, EXETER	In Sight! Lord Dundonald's Dash on Ladysmith
LEAMINGTON Art Gallery and Museum	Winter's White Silence
Walker Art Gallery, LIVERPOOL	Low Tide, St Ives
LONDON	
Imperial War Museum	The Straw Ride, Russley Park Remount Depot Exercise, The Ladies Army Remount Depot, Russley Park, Wiltshire, 1918
Tate Gallery	Colt Hunting in the New Forest Forward the Guns!

Royal Exchange	Women's Work during the Great War 1914-18
ROCHDALE Art Gallery	Hill Folk
Graves Art Gallery SHEFFIELD	The Riders
Atkinson Art Gallery SOUTHPORT	Pencil study of Horses in Harvest Fields
SOUTHAMPTON City Art Gallery	The Head of the Timber Run
AUSTRALIA	
National Gallery of Victoria MELBOURNE	Horses Bathing in the Sea
NEW ZEALAND	
Aigantighe Art Gallery TIMARU	The Wanderers
AUCKLAND City Art Gallery	The Evening Camp
Robert McDougall Art Gallery CHRISTCHURCH	Timber Coming Down the Mountainside, Wales Sunlight through Leaves
Museum of New Zealand WELLINGTON	The Night Cometh
SOUTH AFRICA	
National Gallery of South Africa CAPE TOWN	Calves
Tatham Art Gallery PIETERMARITZBURG	The Village Street
JOHANNESBURG Art Gallery	The Circus Smithy

THE ANTIQUE COLLECTORS' CLUB

The Antique Collectors' Club was formed in 1966 and quickly grew to a five figure membership spread throughout the world. It publishes the only independently run monthly antiques magazine, *Antique Collecting*, which caters for those collectors who are interested in widening their knowledge of antiques, both by greater awareness of quality and by discussion of the factors which influence the price that is likely to be asked. The Antique Collectors' Club pioneered the provision of information on prices for collectors and the magazine still leads in the provision of detailed articles on a variety of subjects.

It was in response to the enormous demand for information on 'what to pay' that the price guide series was introduced in 1968 with the first edition of *The Price Guide to Antique Furniture* (completely revised 1978 and 1989), a book which broke new ground by illustrating the more common types of antique furniture, the sort that collectors could buy in shops and at auctions rather than the rare museum pieces which had previously been used (and still to a large extent are used) to make up the limited amount of illustrations in books published by commercial publishers. Many other price guides have followed, all copiously illustrated, and greatly appreciated by collectors for the valuable information they contain, quite apart from prices. The Price Guide Series heralded the publication of many standard works of reference on art and antiques. *The Dictionary of British Art* (now in six volumes), *The Pictorial Dictionary of British 19th Century Furniture Design, Oak Furniture* and *Early English Clocks* were followed by many deeply researched reference works such as *The Directory of Gold and Silversmiths,* providing new information. Many of these books are now accepted as the standard work of reference on their subject.

The Antique Collectors' Club has widened its list to include books on gardens and architecture. All the Club's publications are available through bookshops world wide and a full catalogue of all these titles is available free of charge from the addresses below.

Club membership, open to all collectors, costs little. Members receive free of charge *Antique Collecting*, the Club's magazine (published ten times a year), which contains well-illustrated articles dealing with the practical aspects of collecting not normally dealt with by magazines. Prices, features of value, investment potential, fakes and forgeries are all given prominence in the magazine.

Among other facilities available to members are private buying and selling facilities, the longest list of 'For Sales' of any antiques magazine, an annual ceramics conference and the opportunity to meet other collectors at their local antique collectors' clubs. There are over eighty in Britain and more than a dozen overseas. Members may also buy the Club's publications at special pre-publication prices.

As its motto implies, the Club is an organisation designed to help collectors get the most out of their hobby: it is informal and friendly and gives enormous enjoyment to all concerned.

For Collectors — By Collectors — About Collecting

ANTIQUE COLLECTORS' CLUB
5 Church Street, Woodbridge Suffolk IP12 1DS, UK
Tel: 01394 385501 Fax: 01394 384434
or
Market Street Industrial Park, Wappingers' Falls, NY 12590, USA
Tel: 914 297 0003 Fax: 914 297 0068